Insights for Sales Force Success

Practical Ideas for Winning in Today's Sales Environment

Andris A. Zoltners

Prabha K. Sinha

Sally E. Lorimer

ZS Associates, Inc.

Published by ZS Associates, Inc.
1800 Sherman Avenue, Suite 700
Evanston, Illinois 60201

www.zsassociates.com

ISBN: 978-0-9853436-7-5

Contents

About the Blogs

Since 2011, ZS co-founders Andy Zoltners and Prabha Sinha and former ZS principal Sally Lorimer have shared their insights on sales force management in blogs written for the Harvard Business Review Blog Network. Through these blogs, the authors have provided sales leaders and managers with timely and practical ideas for addressing the challenges of today's selling environment. The blogs cover a wide range of topics, including the following.

- **Sales strategy:** finding hidden opportunities for sales growth, understanding customer potential, and getting sales and marketing to work better together

- **Sales process and organization design:** aligning sales roles and structure around customer needs, using inside sales channels, and sizing the sales force for profitable growth

- **Sales talent management:** hiring and developing the best salespeople, building a winning sales management team, and understanding and addressing the causes of sales force turnover

- **Motivating and directing sales activity:** creating the right sales force incentives, setting challenging but fair sales goals, and providing value-adding sales tools and information

- **Sales force support:** creating world-class sales operations capabilities, using data and analytics to build strategic advantage, and deploying technology to enhance sales processes and better serve customers

Many of the blog topics were inspired by the thousands of executive students and clients the authors have worked with in a range of industries all over the globe.

The original blogs can be found on **hbr.org** and have also been reproduced for easy access at **info.zsassociates.com/salesforceinsights**.

About Harvard Business Publishing

Harvard Business Publishing was founded in 1994 as a not-for-profit wholly owned subsidiary of Harvard University, reporting to the Harvard Business School. Its mission is to improve the practice of management in a changing world. Learn more at **hbr.org**.

About ZS

ZS is the world's largest firm focused exclusively on helping companies improve overall performance and grow revenue and market share through end-to-end sales and marketing solutions—from customer insights and strategy to analytics, operations, and technology. More than 4,500 ZS professionals in 22 offices worldwide draw on deep industry and domain expertise to deliver impact for clients across multiple industries. To learn more, visit **www.zsassociates.com**.

Acknowledgments

As academics and consultants, we have done a lot of writing over the last four decades. It wasn't until 2011 that we became bloggers, and that is thanks to the encouragement of Dan McGinn and his team at the Harvard Business Press. Dan's edits and suggestions always help improve our blogs and make them accessible to business leaders.

Fortunately, thanks to many, many contributors, we never have a shortage of sales force topics to blog about. Our contributors include the following:

Our executive students. In every class (dating back to 1987 when we began teaching *Accelerating Sales Force Performance* in the executive education program at Northwestern University's Kellogg School of Management), lively classroom discussions among course participants have given us new insights about the challenges of running a sales force and have inspired many of the blog topics in this book.

The people of ZS Associates. The consulting firm that we founded in 1983 employs some of the finest consultants and businesspeople in the world. Several of the ideas and examples in our blogs come directly from ZS consultants, who share with us the wisdom they have gained by working with companies in many industries and situations all over the globe.

The clients of ZS. Our clients (some of whom have been working with us for more than three decades) have allowed us to discover, develop, test, and refine many of the concepts described in our blogs. Because of confidentiality, the specific people and companies must remain nameless, but we are grateful to all those who have helped us cultivate and enhance our ideas.

We were also fortunate to have an exceptional design and production team working with us on this book. Lisa Davis led the book's production and editorial efforts. The ZS Marketing team, including Melanie McKnight and Ganesh Singh, designed the book's layout and cover.

Thank you to all of the fine contributors who have supported and encouraged us in creating this book.

Introduction

Sales Force Success

As your company faces an ever-changing business environment, the sales force needs constant attention and improvement. The issues that arise can come from many sources.

Some sales force issues originate outside the company.

- **Customers.** "Customer needs are changing. As buyers use the Internet and social media to learn about our products and those of our competitors, many are coming into the sales processes better informed than ever before."

- **Competitors.** "Several new global competitors have entered our markets, while one of our longtime competitors has gone out of business."

- **Environment.** "Economic growth, new technologies, and changing government regulations are impacting our customers."

Some issues come from within the company but outside the sales force.

- **Product portfolio.** "Our company is launching a new product that will require the sales force to sell to a different customer base."

- **Mergers and corporate restructuring.** "Our company is reorganizing and plans to merge the sales forces of two formerly separate divisions."

- **Leadership.** "We have a new CEO who has a different philosophy about how to run the sales force."

Some issues arise from observations about various sales force outcomes.

- **Sales strategy.** "We are targeting too many of the wrong customers with an outdated value proposition that no longer resonates."

- **Sales process and organization.** "Sales roles and responsibilities are unclear."

- **Salespeople.** "Too many of our salespeople lack knowledge about customers and products. And we are losing our best salespeople to competitors."

- **Sales activity.** "Salespeople are spending too little time with key decision makers at strategically important accounts. And there is too much non-selling time."

Some issues originate within specific sales force decisions, programs, and processes.

- **Sales force size.** "We need more salespeople to cover our markets."

- **Training.** "We need better training for our sales managers."

- **Quota setting.** "We need to improve the quota-setting process so that quotas are reasonable and fair for everyone."

Finally, some issues focus on results.

- **Customers.** "Customer retention is too low."

- **Company.** "We are not making our sales goals."

Sales Force Complexity

Managing a sales force is no small task. Running a sales force is like running an entire business. Sales force leaders deal with issues ranging from strategy development to managing human resources, logistics, operations, and finance to establishing an organizational culture. Sales forces are complex and have many moving pieces. The complexity is only getting greater in today's technology-enabled world, as information gives customers power in the buying process, and sales process execution involves more coordination among multiple sales roles and digital communication channels. If your mandate is to lead a sales force to "drive profitable sales growth," it's hard to know where to start, especially if you face complex issues such as changing customer needs and expectations, more competition, new company strategies, high turnover of the best salespeople, a complacent sales force, or too little sales force attention focused on strategically important customers or product lines.

A Chain of Sales Force Outcomes

We created this compilation of blogs to help you figure out where to turn. All but a few of the blogs were originally written for the *Harvard Business Review* Blog Network (available at hbr.org). We have organized the blogs around a sales force system framework that centers on a chain of outcomes providing insight for addressing issues and creating sales force success. These outcomes, as illustrated in Figure 1, include a sales strategy, which guides a sales process and organization design, to allow talented and motivated people in the sales force to engage in the right kinds of sales activity for creating value for customers. If all of that happens, a successful sales force ultimately drives company results.

A Chain of Sales Force System Outcomes

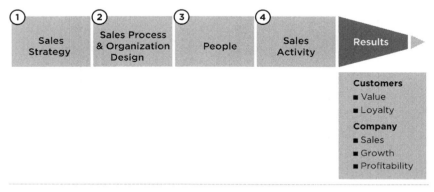

Figure 1. Sales Force System Framework: Chain of Outcomes

The Sales Force Effectiveness Drivers

Sales leaders affect the chain of outcomes (and therefore can address issues and influence sales force success) through their decisions and through the processes, systems, and programs for which they are responsible. We call these the sales force effectiveness drivers, and they are organized into the five categories shown in Figure 2. The first four categories each have primary influence over one of the outcomes within the chain (and sometimes have secondary influence on other outcomes). The fifth category supports and enables the entire chain.

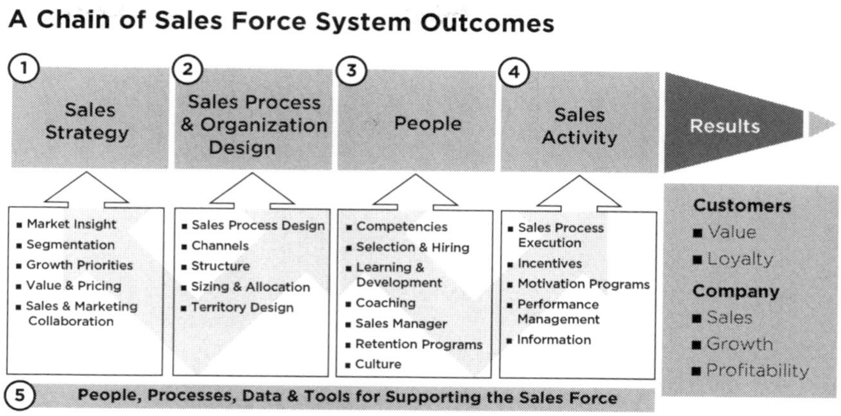

A Chain of Sales Force System Outcomes

Figure 2. Sales Force System Framework: Five Categories of Effectiveness Drivers

The five categories of sales force effectiveness drivers are described here.

1. Sales strategy drivers

Defining who (which customers or market segments) your company will sell to and what you should offer each segment is the starting point for aligning your sales force around the needs of your customers.

- **Market insight:** understanding customer needs, expertise, potential, buying process, and evolution

- **Segmentation:** grouping customers based on profile, potential, penetration, needs, and expertise

- **Growth priorities:** prioritizing sources of growth in markets, products, and salespeople

- **Value and pricing:** defining offerings by segment and the value they bring to customers, and then pricing to reflect that value

- **Sales and marketing collaboration:** creating processes for sales and marketing to collaborate and communicate to develop and implement strategies for delivering value to customers and realizing value for the company

2. Sales process and organization design drivers
A structural blueprint for the sales force lays out the steps for delivering value to customers, the channels and sales roles that will execute those steps, and the size and deployment of the sales team.

- **Sales process design:** defining the stages of selling, consisting of key activities, milestones, roles, and enablers

- **Channels:** selecting the right resources (e.g., direct sales, selling partners, inside sales, e-channels) for creating effective and efficient customer connections

- **Structure:** assigning products, customer segments, and activities to sales teams, and defining sales force reporting relationships

- **Sizing and allocation:** sizing the sales teams and allocating effort to products, customers, and activities

- **Territory design:** assigning individual customers and geographies to salespeople, considering workload and potential

3. People drivers
Unquestionably the heart of any sales force, the right sales and managerial talent must be developed to excel at delivering the strategy in the defined structure.

- **Competencies:** defining the role-specific characteristics and competencies that people need to sell and succeed

- **Selection and hiring:** creating recruiting profiles, target candidate pools, evaluation processes, and programs for selecting and attracting job candidates

- **Learning and development:** continuously improving sales force skills on products, customers, sales processes, and markets

- **Coaching:** enabling sales managers to enhance salespeople's capabilities during field visits

- **Sales manager:** hiring, developing, and supporting sales managers in people management, customer, and business management roles

- **Retention programs:** providing programs that energize and retain the good salespeople at every career stage

- **Culture:** creating and reinforcing an unwritten set of rules that guide sales force behavior

4. Sales activity drivers

For people on the sales team to execute the sales strategy in the defined structure, they must deliver a high quantity and quality of sales effort, allocated to the right products, markets, and selling tasks.

■ **Sales process execution:** organizing the sales pipeline, and targeting and managing customers and prospects

■ **Incentives:** linking compensation to results to motivate and direct salespeople and managers

■ **Motivation programs:** providing motivation and recognition programs, role clarity, leadership, and empowerment to motivate employees

■ **Performance management:** setting goals, monitoring, and giving feedback to sustain and enhance performance

■ **Information:** providing information that helps salespeople, managers, and leaders make better decisions

5. Sales force support drivers

Having impact across the entire chain of sales force system outcomes, certain capabilities support ongoing sales force needs and help bring excellence to all the sales force effectiveness drivers.

■ **People:** providing a range of people and expertise using employees and partners to support and design the many sales force effectiveness drivers, guided by strong sales operations leadership

■ **Processes:** having the processes to accomplish the support and design work efficiently and effectively

■ **Data and tools:** using data and technology to enable the processes and create insights for enhancing sales force performance

Sales Force Solutions

Companies can use the sales force system framework to identify solutions for the issues they face. Whether those issues originate in the market (e.g., evolving customer needs), within the company (e.g., a new corporate strategy), or within the sales force (e.g., a complacent sales team), the solution is almost always in the sales force effectiveness drivers.

Consider, for example, the issue that a technology sales force faced. The company was not achieving its sales goal for a strategically important new product. Salespeople were not allocating enough selling time to the product; instead, they were spending too much time selling familiar and easy-to-sell products and calling on low-stress "friends and family" accounts.

The company used the sales force system framework to organize an assessment of the situation. As shown in Figure 3, the diagnosis began with a series of five questions aimed at identifying the probable root causes of the problem. This led to the discovery of solutions within the sales force effectiveness drivers.

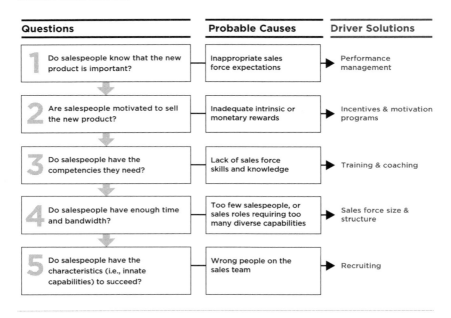

Figure 3. *Diagnosing a New Product Performance Issue at a Technology Company*

The diagnosis revealed that salespeople did in fact understand the importance of the new product to the company (question 1). But answers to questions 2 through 5 showed multiple reasons that salespeople were under-supporting the new product, and this led the company to a multifaceted solution.

■ **Incentives.** Salespeople were not motivated to sell the new product. They found it complex and hard to sell, and they could earn more money by focusing on familiar products. The company adjusted the sales incentive plan to pay a higher commission rate on sales of the new product and a lower rate on other products.

- **Training and coaching.** Salespeople felt inadequately prepared to respond to customer concerns and questions about the new product. The company revamped its sales training program to focus on the new competencies needed to sell the product, and they provided sales managers with additional support for coaching salespeople on how to sell the new product.

- **Size and structure.** Salespeople said they had too much on their plates already and didn't have time to master the technical details of the new product. The company added a new specialist sales role for the product, giving salespeople a resource for bringing expertise to customers.

- **Hiring.** Successful selling of the new product required a level of technical capability that some of the current salespeople simply didn't possess. The company created a new hiring profile with the additional characteristics that were needed for success with the new product.

Together, these changes brought about the change in sales force behavior that the company desired, increased sales of the new product, and enhanced the company's competitiveness in the market.

Almost always, the answer for addressing issues, solving problems, or capitalizing on opportunities in a sales force can be found in the sales force effectiveness drivers. To create a successful sales force, look to the five categories of drivers.

Link the issue you face back to the drivers. Use the sales force system framework to guide your diagnosis. Ask questions to help you identify the probable cause of your situation. Link the cause to remedies in the sales force effectiveness drivers, and modify the drivers to bring about a solution.

Implement best practices and continually improve. Build the best possible capability around the sales force effectiveness drivers. Devote resources to ensuring that the sales strategy is sound, the organization is well designed, the processes for acquiring and developing talent are excellent, and the tools and programs for motivating and enhancing sales team performance are world-class. Learn what works and what doesn't by observing your best salespeople, and use that learning to bring about improvement. Invest in continuously upgrading the sales force effectiveness drivers that have the greatest impact on the issues you face.

Align all of the drivers with one another and with company business strategies. Ensure alignment and compatibility across all the sales force effectiveness drivers. For example, if the sales strategy calls for penetrating a new market segment, make sure that the strategy is enabled with the right sales process, an appropriate sales force size and structure, training and coaching programs, and data and tools that facilitate salespeople's success. Make all of the drivers work consistently together to support company goals and strategies.

By building capability and alignment across the sales force effectiveness drivers, you create excellence across the entire chain of outcomes: a sales strategy that guides an effective and efficient sales process and organization that allows talented and motivated people to engage in high levels of the right kinds of sales activity for creating value for customers. If all of that happens, the sales force ultimately drives company results. And that is our definition of sales force success.

Sales Force Success Blogs

The following blogs share general insights about how effectiveness across the entire chain of sales force system outcomes is essential for driving results.

Are You Paying Enough Attention To Your Sales Force?

There's a question all top managers should ask: how can I make my sales force, which is one of the biggest and most important investments my company makes, perform more effectively?

There are several reasons this question is so important.

Sales forces are expensive. Despite predictions by some pundits that many sales jobs would disappear due to the Internet and "big data," companies continue to invest in sales forces in a big way. According to *Selling Power* magazine (July/August/September 2012 issue), the largest companies in America—selling products such as computer and office equipment, consumable goods, insurance, telecommunications, and financial services—each employ tens of thousands of salespeople. By our estimates, the amount invested in U.S. sales forces in 2012 exceeds $800 billion a year. This is 4.7 times the estimated $169.5 billion spent on all media advertising in 2012 and more than 20 times the estimated $39.5 billion spent on Internet advertising in 2012.

Sales forces are empowered. The significance of a sales force goes beyond its cost. The sales force is perhaps the most highly empowered organization within most companies. Usually working alone and unsupervised, salespeople are entrusted with a company's most important asset—its relationship with its customers. To many customers, the salesperson is the company. As customers face a proliferation of buying choices, the way a company sells becomes a key point of competitive differentiation and a source of customer value. This makes an effective sales force essential for driving top-line performance.

Sales force dynamics are complex and poorly understood. Managing a sales force requires many difficult decisions. For example, you need a sales strategy defining which customers to target, what value proposition to offer, and what sales process to use to engage customers and create mutual value. You need to decide what sales force size and structure best allow you to meet customer needs and achieve company goals. You need to choose whom to hire for the sales team and decide how to continually develop sales team skills and knowledge. And you need to determine the goals, incentives, and sales culture that will motivate peak sales force effort and performance.

Many companies today are taking a more strategic and data-driven approach to making all of these and other sales force decisions. But regrettably, our understanding of what drives sales force success still falls short when compared to the cost of a sales force and the huge impact that salespeople have on customers and company performance. Sales continues to be one of the most poorly understood and under-optimized areas of business. Compared to marketing, the number of good books and academic articles on sales force topics is woefully inadequate. In the last 10 years, only 3 percent of the articles in four leading academic journals (*Marketing Science, Harvard Business Review, Journal of Marketing*, and *Journal of Marketing Research*) have focused on sales force topics. In 2009 (the last year that one of this blog's authors taught MBA students at the Kellogg School of Management at Northwestern), the graduating class left the university having taken over 4,000 course equivalents on marketing topics—but only 100 course equivalents on sales. Less than 1 percent of undergraduate institutions in the United States offer a major or minor in sales, and none of the top 20 graduate business schools offer a concentration in sales for their MBA students. (*The Harvard Business Review* ran an article on the dearth of academic programs in sales in its July/August 2012 issue.)

Improving sales force management is a huge opportunity. We believe that sales force improvement initiatives typically produce incremental short-term revenue gains of at least 10 percent and long-term increases of 50 percent or more. Consider the following examples of companies that have implemented sales force improvement initiatives that had big positive impacts on the bottom line.

- A business within GE that leases over-the-road trailers sought to refocus sales efforts to improve productivity. Leaders invested to develop better measures of customer potential. In just one year, qualified leads increased by 33 percent. The customer-potential data also helped GE redeploy several sales territories into more lucrative markets, allowing the business to grow sales productivity by 7 percent without adding people.

- Global healthcare company Novartis identified a group of outstanding performers in its U.S. sales force, and isolated a set of "success principles" and behaviors that differentiated their performance. Leaders developed a new sales process based on these success principles and behaviors, and aligned sales hiring, development, and other programs to support the new process. The initiative contributed to six consecutive years of double-digit top-line growth, well above the industry average.

- Temporary housing provider Oakwood Worldwide transformed its sales force to align better with customers' need for a more consultative sales approach. This involved a new sales force hiring profile, training program, coaching process, and sales enablement tools and metrics. A large percentage of the sales force did not survive the transformation, but most top performers did. A year after implementation, deal win rates had tripled, sales cycle time had dropped by 50 percent, and salesperson turnover had declined to under 5 percent.

More research and education on sales and continued work to develop and refine frameworks for understanding the drivers of sales force effectiveness can make a significant business impact in the years to come.

This blog was first published on April 12, 2013, on the Harvard Business Review web site: **https://hbr.org/2013/04/are-you-paying-enough-attention-to**

Silver Bullets Won't Fix Your Sales Force

When it comes to enhancing sales force productivity and performance, it's tempting to look for silver bullets. Is customer retention declining? Okay, let's roll out a new sales training program that teaches salespeople how to be more customer-focused. Is sales growth lagging? Let's implement a more aggressive incentive plan to motivate the sales force. Is sales productivity decreasing? Let's build a big data solution that enables salespeople to glean insights so they can sell smarter.

One-dimensional solutions like these are rarely enough to create permanent improvements in sales force effectiveness. A sales force is complex, with many moving parts and interdependencies. Achieving sales force excellence, or addressing a sales opportunity or challenge (such as revitalizing growth or enhancing customer retention), typically requires improving on a mixture of several sales force effectiveness drivers.

Instead of simplistic, one-note fixes, smart managers consider broader improvement plans, such as the following.

- Set a cohesive sales strategy that focuses sales effort on the right customer segments with a compelling value proposition.

- Design a high-impact sales process for communicating and delivering value to customers.

- Size the sales organization at a profitable investment level that provides ideal customer coverage

- Define a sales structure and sales roles that enable effectiveness (high sales for the effort) as well as efficiency (low cost for the effort).

- Assign accounts to salespeople to enable good customer coverage and give all salespeople a fair chance to succeed.

- Hire sales talent by identifying and attracting salespeople with the characteristics (innate capabilities and values) that drive success.

- Train and coach that talent to continually develop the competencies (learned skills and knowledge) that salespeople need to add value for customers.

- Provide data, tools, and resources for enhancing sales force insight about customers and supporting the sales process.

- Offer incentive compensation and recognition programs that encourage salespeople to work hard in pursuit of personal goals that align with company goals.

- Set sales force goals that are challenging, fair, and well understood by the sales force.

- Manage performance by engaging a team of first-line sales managers who can effectively direct sales activity and keep the sales force on course.

- Create and sustain a sales culture of accountability, achievement, and ethics.

These sales force effectiveness drivers are the spokes of a wheel that powers the sales force. Breakage in any single spoke creates weakness in the wheel, leading to suboptimal results. Excellent sales forces continuously improve capability around every sales force effectiveness driver through "kaizen." They devote organizational resources to making every sales force efficiency driver excellent—from formulating the right sales strategy, to hiring and developing talent, to providing the best tools, programs, and resources for motivating and enhancing sales team performance.

Excellent sales forces also ensure compatibility across these types of programs. For example, if sales strategy calls for penetrating a new market segment, the company enables the strategy with the right sales process, an appropriate sales force size and structure, training and coaching programs, and data and tools that facilitate salespeople's success. If salespeople have unequal market potential, the company designs performance management and incentive programs that account for territory differences, or it realigns territories to give all salespeople a fair opportunity to succeed.

As sales leaders face an ever-changing market, this laundry list of drivers of sales force efficiency—a list of activities that require constant attention and improvement—can look daunting. That's where a clear head and a purposeful prioritization process come in handy. We suggest that you rethink a few key of these drivers at any point in time.

Some drivers can be changed fairly easily without significant disruption to the sales force—for example, performance management, data and tools, training, and incentives. But if you are rethinking your sales model, you'll likely need to plan for some disruption to salespeople and customers as you redefine some of the more strategic drivers, such as sales strategy, sales process, structure, size, and even the profile of people you need to hire.

There are no silver bullets in building and sustaining a high-performance sales force. Rather, it's a lot of blocking and tackling. Only by managing the entire portfolio of sales force efficiency drivers and building capability and compatibility throughout the system, can you drive sustained sales force effectiveness and top- and bottom-line performance.

This blog was first published on October 9, 2012, on the Harvard Business Review web site: **http://blogs.hbr.org/cs/2012/10/what_really_improves_a_sales_force.html**

Improving Your Sales Force: Fine-Tune or Transform?

In the continuous hunt for profitable growth, silver bullets won't fix your sales force. The solutions to most sales force challenges are multi-dimensional. Especially when things are not going well (and sometimes even when they are), sales leaders need to know when evolutionary sales force improvements are enough to drive profitable growth, and when it's necessary to implement a wholesale sales force transformation.

Most evolutionary changes work within the current sales strategy, organizational structure, and sales team. The focus is on getting current sales team members to behave differently. For example, to spend more (or less) time prospecting, to improve customer engagement quality, or to manage the pipeline more effectively. Several operational levers influence sales team activity to help you achieve these ends, including the following.

- **Performance management:** setting expectations and managing against them

- **Data and tools:** providing salespeople with insights that enable success with customers

- **Incentives:** motivating high levels of the right sales activity

- **Training and coaching:** helping salespeople develop the competencies they need

Evolutionary improvements can also involve minor adjustments to sales strategy (e.g., focusing more effort on specific market segments), tweaks to sales force size or structure (e.g., closing a vacant territory in a low-growth market), or small modifications to hiring profiles (e.g., screening candidates on technology skills). But major changes to these more strategic levers require you to graduate your sales force improvement efforts to a more disruptive, transformational change of your sales model and the people on the sales team. Examples include the following.

- **Sales process:** implementing a major change to the sales process, such as a move from a relationship-based sales process to a consultative sales process

- **Salesperson profile and recruiting:** recruiting a different profile of salesperson and eliminating people on the current team who don't fit the new profile

- **Sales force structure and scale:** specializing (or unspecializing) the sales force or significantly increasing or reducing its size, resulting in major realignment of salesperson-customer relationships

Transformational change typically requires a makeover of operational sales force levers as well (e.g., performance management, data and tools, incentives, training and coaching) to keep sales activity aligned within the new sales model.

Sales forces have realized significant performance improvements through evolutionary and transformational change initiatives. Here are two examples.

Evolutionary improvement: Healthcare company Novartis operationalized evolutionary improvement by conducting annual sales force effectiveness reviews. The reviews led to initiatives such as improving customer-targeting approaches and enhancing development programs, coaching tools, and performance management processes to reflect the behaviors of top-performing salespeople. These evolutionary improvements contributed to six consecutive years of double-digit top-line growth in the United States, well above the industry average. Many of the improvements were also implemented globally.

Transformational change: Temporary housing provider Oakwood Worldwide implemented a sales force transformation to address changing customer needs that necessitated a move from a relationship-based sales approach to a consultative sales approach. It designed a new sales process around the best practices of top-performing salespeople. A large percentage of the sales force did not survive the transformation, but most top performers did. The transformation was supported by changes to operational levers such as sales training programs, coaching processes, and sales enablement tools and metrics. A year after implementation, deal win rates had tripled, sales cycle time had dropped by 50 percent, and salesperson turnover had declined to under 5 percent.

Transformational change is usually the best option when customer and company results are seriously threatened or when an opportunity or environmental factor dictates a drastic rewrite of the sales process. This is easiest to do when you face a crucial event—such as a merger or acquisition, a new company strategy, a major new product launch, a missed financial goal, a change in company leadership, or a major market shift—that acts as a catalyst for change. Transformational change frequently results in a short-term dip in performance, even when done right. You'll get the best results if during the transition you take steps to protect your top customers and any top salespeople who are well suited to succeed in the new sales model.

The best sales forces make evolutionary improvements all the time.

This blog was first published on November 13, 2012, on the Harvard Business Review web site:
http://blogs.hbr.org/cs/2012/11/improving_your_sales_force_fin.html

Help Your Salespeople Spend Time on the Right Things

Sales executives typically have two levers to try to increase sales: they can increase the *quantity* of sales effort by adding salespeople, or they can improve the *quality* of sales effort by investing in coaching and training.

There is a third approach that is often overlooked: improving the *allocation* of sales effort. Salespeople can work smarter, not harder, by dividing their time more appropriately among customers, products, and sales activities. Sales effort allocation has a large impact on sales and profits, sometimes more than increasing the quantity and/or quality of effort.

Sales executives frequently talk about how sales forces misallocate effort. Salespeople spend too much time with "friends and family" (existing customers with whom they have rapport) instead of focusing on high-potential prospects. Strategically important products don't get sufficient sales support. Service or other nonsales activities creep into the sales job, and role pollution prevents salespeople from developing new business. Costly allocation errors such as these are difficult to diagnose and fix.

By asking six questions (in order below from the simplest to the most complex), you can trace the probable cause of any sales effort misallocation back to the sales force decisions and programs that can bring about improvement.

1. **Do salespeople know what's important?** If salespeople aren't clear about which markets and products are priorities, they'll create their own rules about how to spend time. The remedy is clear and consistent communication: "Here's how we want you to spend your time, and here are the results we expect." Coaching, performance management, and sales goals reinforce communication, while metrics track performance: "What gets measured gets done." When a business logistics company wanted salespeople to spend more time selling three strategic product lines, it focused sales force attention on those lines by giving salespeople a sales goal for each line, separate from their goal for the overall portfolio. Salespeople could track up-to-the-minute achievement of all goals.

2. **Do salespeople have the information they need?** Salespeople are more likely to spend time effectively when they have access to good information and tools. A telecom company used predictive models (think Netflix and Amazon) to give salespeople direction about how to improve sales with underperforming, high-potential customers. By finding "data doubles" for these customers—that is, similar customers who were buying much more—the company provided salespeople with insights about which underperforming customers had significant unrealized opportunity and which sales strategies had worked in comparable situations in the past. The information helped salespeople focus on product offerings that matched customer needs, thus increasing sales.

3. **Do salespeople have the competencies required?** When salespeople neglect priorities due to insufficient skills and knowledge, the remedy is coaching and training. A computer manufacturer selling through resellers discovered that many of the resellers' salespeople weren't sufficiently supporting the manufacturer's new product, resulting in low sales and lost opportunity. The manufacturer's product training for the resellers' salespeople emphasized technology specifications. This worked for the best and most experienced salespeople but left others overwhelmed and unprepared to approach customers. When the manufacturer refocused the training around how to sell the product (e.g., how to find and qualify buyers, describe the product's competitive advantages, and show customers why they should buy), the resellers' salespeople became more confident, and sales increased.

4. **Are salespeople motivated to succeed?** Salespeople are motivated when they perceive value from their efforts: career success, recognition, personal satisfaction, money, or all of the above. Remedies for sales force motivation issues include changing the incentive plan and/or modifying the criteria for recognition programs while acknowledging those who are successful. When a medical instruments manufacturer wanted to build market share by displacing a specific competitor, it offered salespeople a bonus for every competitive instrument displaced, and it set up a mobile app with a leaderboard of salespeople with the most displacements. First-line sales managers also helped boost motivation by encouraging salespeople and recognizing their successes.

5. **Do salespeople have enough bandwidth?** When salespeople spend time inappropriately because they have too many diverse responsibilities, a new sales force structure can ensure focus on company priorities. When new customer development lagged at a technology company, it reorganized the sales force into a hunter/farmer structure. Hunters specialized in developing new accounts. Once a sale was made, a farmer took over to cultivate and grow the relationship and generate repeat business. Farmers provided existing customers with the ongoing support they needed, while new business development flourished because hunters were not distracted by time-consuming service activities.

6. **Do salespeople have the right innate characteristics?** Training can develop salespeople's competencies, but success can also require certain innate qualities. When sales effort misallocation occurs because salespeople lack characteristics such as intellectual flexibility or tenacity, the remedy is better hiring and retaining the right people. A construction supply distributor historically hired former construction workers for its sales force. Many of these salespeople had technical expertise but lacked the personality, capability, and drive to sell in challenging situations. When the economy slowed, selling became more difficult, and salespeople started focusing almost exclusively on friendly, loyal customers. The distributor changed its hiring strategy: instead of hiring industry experts, it began hiring "natural sellers" who were willing to learn the industry. The change, when reinforced by other changes to the sales culture, drove considerable revenue improvement.

These questions are sequenced so that those asked first can be addressed with easier-to-implement sales force changes. Changes to performance metrics and information (questions 1 and 2) typically require moderate effort and minimal disruption. Changes to sales force structure and hiring (questions 5 and 6) are disruptive, are more difficult to implement, and take longer to have an impact. Changes to sales training and incentives (questions 3 and 4) are in the middle. Some effort allocation issues are remedied with only easy changes, but many will require a portfolio of changes to create lasting improvement.

This blog was first published on February 15, 2016, on the Harvard Business Review web site: **https://hbr.org/2016/02/help-your-salespeople-spend-time-on-the-right-things?**

How More-Accessible Information Is Forcing B2B Sales to Adapt

Over the past 20 years, information technology and digital channels have changed the way consumers shop for products ranging from cars to homes to electronics. Those forces are dramatically changing the way B2B companies and their customers approach buying and selling too.

Business buyers are more connected and informed than ever before. Sellers must respond. For buyers and sellers alike, this creates complexity, anxiety, and opportunity all at the same time.

From the buyer's perspective, information technology and digital channels provide access to information and enable self-sufficiency. When a buyer wants to learn about virtually any product or service, an Internet search yields thousands (if not millions) of results, including online articles, videos, white papers, blogs, and social media posts. In addition to supplier web sites that showcase specific solutions, there are likely to be online sources (ranging from the self-serving to the unbiased) to help buyers learn and compare solution alternatives. Buyers can also use self-service digital channels for new or repeat purchases and for training and support. Using information technology and digital channels, buyers can take over many of the buying steps that salespeople once cherished as their source of value.

Buyers are at different levels of self-sufficiency: any single buyer can be at one level for some purchases and at a different level for others. Sometimes buyers prefer to eliminate the salesperson completely. According to one corporate technology buyer: "Our supplier's customized self-service purchasing portal makes it easy to place reorders, track shipping, and return products hassle-free." Other times buyers seek help from salespeople. The same corporate buyer relies on salespeople when evaluating new technologies: "It's more efficient to work with a few trusted salespeople, compared to spending hours on my own sifting through all the information and misinformation that's out there."

Because of the diversity of buyer self-sufficiency, the traditional methods sellers use to customize their selling approach for customers are no longer enough. Considering factors such as customer potential and needs is still relevant. But today, customer knowledge/self-sufficiency is a growing driver of how customers want to buy. At one end of the spectrum are the "super-expert" customers, skilled in gathering information from many sources and self-sufficient in using that information to make purchase decisions. At the other end of the spectrum are the "information-seeking" customers, who want help with examining and evaluating the plethora of information. Many customers are in between these two extremes or are at different points at different times or for different purchases.

Smart sellers match their selling approach to the customer's level of buying knowledge and self-sufficiency. For example, when leaders at Dow Corning observed in the early 2000s that some customers wanted an easier, more affordable way to buy standard silicone products, they created Xiameter, a brand that includes thousands of less-differentiated products sold exclusively through a low-cost, no-frills, self-service online sales channel. Customers who desired a higher-touch approach could still purchase products under the Dow Corning brand name, which also includes specialty silicones backed by research and technical services.

As sellers need a more customized approach to reaching customers, they have a big arsenal of data and technology at their disposal. Systems (e.g., CRM), tools (e.g., data management, analytics), infrastructures (e.g., mobile, cloud), and information (e.g., big data) give sellers knowledge about buyers and enable sales force members to make smarter decisions. And sellers who once connected with customers primarily through personal selling can now use an array of digital communication channels to supplement or supplant face-to-face sales efforts.

Consider the impact of information technology and digital channels from the seller's perspective. Here are examples from several industries.

- **Finding banking customers.** "Social media allows us to cost-effectively reach out to more prospects and showcase our services."

- **Understanding specialty chemicals customers.** "Big data and analytics help us improve customer targeting and achieve more cost-effective deployment."

- **Acquiring advertising customers.** "We now have richer demographic information to help us create more powerful sales messages, resulting in more sales."

- **Serving and growing business logistics customers.** "Our salespeople use a business review app to guide quarterly account reviews with major customers. By sharing data about performance and cost savings, these discussions enhance customer value and retention."

Information technology and digital channels can help sellers become more effective and efficient, but they can also be a source of disharmony and confusion if implemented without thought. Too many sellers have wasted millions of dollars on sales technologies such as CRM systems and data warehouses that never lived up to their potential.

Success for sellers requires many sales force changes beyond information technology and digital solutions. To start, salespeople need new competencies. Customers are no longer interested in meeting with "talking brochures," so salespeople must do more than share product information. They must adapt to each customer's level of knowledge and self-sufficiency. They must use email, social media, webinars, videoconferencing, and other tools judiciously to maximize their own productivity and make the process more efficient for buyers. They must help their companies coordinate customer outreach across multiple communication channels to ensure buyers get a well-orchestrated and consistent message.

For example, in the pharmaceutical industry, gone are the days when the majority of physician education occurred through face-to-face contact between salespeople and physicians. Companies are now tracking individual physician communication preferences and are reaching out with the combination of face-to-face visits and digital methods that best meets each physician's needs. Salespeople need competencies as orchestrators who can ensure an effective and efficient connection.

Developing new sales force competencies is just a start. Sales leaders must also reengineer their sales forces by implementing changes across the entire range of sales force decisions: roles, size and structure, hiring, training, coaching, incentive compensation, performance management, and sales support systems.

This blog was first published on January 6, 2016, on the Harvard Business Review web site: **https://hbr.org/2016/01/how-more-accessible-information-is-forcing-b2b-sales-to-adapt**

Despite Dire Predictions, Salespeople Aren't Going Away

One hundred years ago, an article in *The New York Times* asked a provocative question: "Are salesmen needless?" In the article, a marketing expert explains why societal shifts would render the door-to-door salesman obsolete. "Advertising is producing better results than the old method of personal solicitation," the article reported. "Things were different once upon a time before the railroads turned farms into cities... The traveling [sales] man is a middleman and the evolution of business is gradually eliminating the middle man."

That 1916 prediction didn't prove true. Over the next 50 years, sales force numbers kept expanding—but even as they did, pundits kept predicting the field of sales would soon enter a decline. In the 1962 book *The Vanishing Salesman*, author E.B. Weiss wrote about the "new age of self-selection and self-service" and how preselling, branding, and advertising would eliminate the need for traditional salesmen. (To his credit, Weiss also predicted that sales roles would not die, but would change in some industries.) Yet the number of salespeople continued to grow.

Fast forward to 2015. Forrester Research predicted that one million B2B salespeople will become obsolete by 2020, lost to e-commerce. Is this another doomed prediction? Or are things fundamentally different this time? Will there really be fewer B2B salespeople in 2020?

No doubt, some companies will have fewer salespeople four years from now. But other companies will have more salespeople—and history helps explain why.

Buyers have relied on salespeople to help them through their buying journey for centuries. In the early days of the United States, buyers (often farmers) in need of household goods relied on traveling salesmen for every step of buying. Buyers usually first became aware of new products when a traveling salesman showed up at the door. Buyers used the salesman's help to evaluate what products to purchase, especially for new technologies like clocks and sewing machines. Buyers would purchase directly from the salesman, and relied on the salesman to fulfill the order by delivering the goods on wagon or horseback.

Over the years, innovations in distribution, media, and technology have enabled buyers to use non-sales force channels for various steps of their buying journey. In the early 20th century, advances in transportation, storage, and distribution largely took the task of physical fulfillment of goods away from salespeople. In the late 20th century, a proliferation of media options made buyers aware of products before talking to a salesperson, more so in B2C, but also in B2B markets. Innovation eliminated certain responsibilities for salespeople; yet at the same time, new responsibilities emerged, and entirely new kinds of companies and industries formed.

Today, buyers increasingly use the web to evaluate purchase options in both B2C and B2B markets. Specifically in B2B, buyers will reference web pages, online articles, videos, whitepapers, blogs, and social media resources (both inside and outside of their own company). Enabled by the Internet, corporate buyers can understand and compare products and decide what to buy, often without the help of a salesperson.

But this doesn't mean there will be fewer B2B salespeople. As certain buying steps move from salespeople to online and other channels, new complexities and uncertainties for buyers will emerge. As in the past, innovation within companies and across entire industries will continue to produce new offerings and new ways to buy that are not yet apparent to buyers. This knowledge gap will create a need for salespeople to help buyers navigate unknown waters, even in today's environment.

For example, between 1995 and 2013, the top five pharmaceutical companies shed more than 55% of their salespeople in the United States. But in that same time period, new companies added salespeople. Google created thousands of sales jobs, including a huge inside sales team to sell locally-targeted online advertising to small businesses. Dell added thousands of salespeople as well, as it sought to help customers understand the changing world of technology and make complex purchases involving hardware, software and services. The total number of B2B sales jobs did not shrink.

We expect this dynamic to continue between now and 2020. Yes, hundreds of B2B sales jobs will get eliminated as e-commerce plays a larger role in straightforward buying steps and for well-understood products. But as complexity and uncertainty decline in some situations, new complexity and uncertainty get introduced elsewhere. Especially for business-critical buying decisions, this elevates the importance of salespeople. Companies such as Facebook, industries such as cloud services, and the many hundreds of B2B SAAS (software as a service) startups are furiously adding salespeople.

With the accelerated pace of innovation and new venture formation today, we believe that barring a significant economic downturn, the total number of B2B sales jobs is more likely to grow than shrink over the next several years. In the modern economy, complexity and uncertainty aren't going away.

This blog was first published on March 31, 2016, on the Harvard Business Review web site: **https://hbr.org/2016/03/despite-dire-predictions-salespeople-arent-going-away**

Frugal Sales

Beginning in countries such as India, frugal innovation has taken hold by reducing the complexity and cost of products as diverse as EKG machines, refrigerators, prosthetics, and phones. Coming out of the same world of hyper-competition and extreme frugality, we are seeing the emergence of frugal sales, a way to build and operate a sales organization at high scale, low cost and great simplicity.

To understand what frugal sales is all about, we spoke with Manish Pant, Managing Director of Luminous Power Technologies. Founded in 1988 by Rakesh Malhotra, Luminous Power Technologies is a leading company in the inverter and power storage markets in India. Targeted at households and businesses having access to power for only a few hours a day, often at random times, a typical Luminous system stores energy during times of power availability, and the inverter converts it back to the desired voltage to power lights and fans when the power goes off. In May 2011, Schneider Electric, a global specialist in energy management, acquired a 74 percent stake in Luminous, and Pant of Schneider Electric took over as managing director of Luminous.

Mr. Pant, why do you need frugal sales?

In India, the US$265 cost of a typical inverter and battery combination is a large part of a customer's income. Our customers are extremely value conscious, and they are looking for products that are affordable and reliable. What good is frugal innovation if we match it up with an inflated sales and distribution system? Also remember, every successful competitor is keeping sales frugal too.

What does frugal sales mean for Luminous?

First we have a lean structure with a sales team of 400 covering India and our 1,200 distributors and 50,000 dealers.

Second, we recruit and develop our selling partners to keep the whole system efficient and effective. For regional distribution, we could use outside logistics companies that specialize in C & F (carrying and forwarding). Instead, we take our successful local distributors and elevate them as our exclusive C

& F agents. They are familiar with our products and with the local market and retailers. They are more than distribution partners: they take on some of the sales and promotion roles as well. This boosts revenues, and it shaves a few points off our costs too. We have high loyalty among our employees and partners, which lowers recruiting and on-boarding costs. Much of our dealer network consists of people who started with nothing. We have grown together as people and businesses.

Third, we make sure our infrastructure is efficient. For example, we could rent office space in Gurgaon for $1.25 per square foot per month. We opt instead to be in Janakpuri for $0.50 per square foot.

Fourth, we make sure that everyone in sales has a direct connection to the customer at the ground level so as to ensure relevance, flexibility, and agility. I will give you a typical scenario. There is a regional power cut. The demand for our systems skyrockets. We have to react quickly and make sure everyone in our sales and distribution network is focused on boosting supply within 24 hours. Our leanness means that our people have their fingers on the pulse of the market. Our agility means that we can move rapidly.

Finally, and underlying it all, is a culture and mind-set of extreme frugality. Everything has to be as functional and lean as our products: structure, people, partners, processes, infrastructure, systems.

Now that Schneider Electric owns 74 percent of Luminous, will not the added systems and processes kill the frugality?

We plan to keep the Schneider Electric and the Luminous brands with their separate identities in India. Luminous and Sachin Tendulkar, its brand ambassador, are known and trusted. We want to leverage that. And we don't want the process and PowerPoint mind-set to overpower the passion, frugality, and agility at Luminous.

But surely, there are financial controls and compliance and transparency norms at Schneider that you will bring to Luminous?

No doubt this is happening. When it comes to safety, the environment, and compliance, there is no compromise. I will give you an example. If a battery label says 1,000 VA, some might interpret this to mean that it should be within 5 percent of this (which means at least 950 VA) 90 percent of the time. The Schneider Electric standards are much higher. And that's what we will go with.

Some costs will go up. We have to be vigilant to make sure that just as many go down. We have streamlined credit and collections, and this has made us even leaner. We have added capabilities in HR, Marketing, and Research in order to enhance our scalability and sustainability and to de-risk the business.

Luminous has always believed in empowerment of its sales managers and salespeople. For example, we have local expense budgets under the control of our sales managers. We now bring discipline to it by setting some boundary conditions on how the money can be spent, and we have transparency requirements so that they have to document the local spending. But the decision still rests with the manager, and we now have insights into what works so that we can spread the word. Keep the passion and empowerment; strengthen it with a light process.

Where does frugal sales go from here for you?

Three things. First, we will keep our focus on frugality and agility at Luminous. Second, we have merged our Schneider retail electrical products business into Luminous, where the retail and frugality DNA lives. We will be escalating the product portfolio in this area. Third, many, many emerging markets can benefit from what we have learned. We are already taking this model to countries such as Nigeria and Indonesia.

This blog was written in November 2013.

Section 1

Sales Strategy

Sales force success starts with a sales strategy that targets the right markets and market segments for realizing growth opportunities with a differentiated and valuable offering.

The blogs in this section share insights about how to develop a winning sales strategy.

How to Spot Hidden Opportunities for Sales Growth

In the hunt for sales growth, profit growth, or share growth from the sales force, every sales leader, whether new or seasoned, whether from a growth-stage or a mature-stage company, faces the same question: where will the growth come from?

The best answers are frequently unearthed by looking at differences in performance, sales activity, and market potential across different pieces of the business—certain customer segments, selected products within a broad portfolio, or specific groups of salespeople. Better analytics, as well as improved data storage and organization technologies, are enabling companies to get more creative in how they analyze data to discover and take advantage of these hidden pockets of growth.

Here are several examples.

Novartis got more out of its average performers. Working first with the U.S. sales force, global healthcare company Novartis identified a group of salespeople who were outstanding performers and isolated a set of behaviors that differentiated their performance from that of average performers. The company developed a new sales process that was derived from the behaviors of the outstanding performers, and it aligned sales hiring, development, and other programs to support the new process. A key part of the initiative was a selling skills–training program called Performance Frontier—The Next Generation in Sales Excellence. In a controlled study, newly trained previously "average" salespeople realized twice the growth rate in sales when compared to a control group of "average" salespeople who were not trained on the newly identified behaviors. Based on this success, Novartis replicated the approach globally.

A manufacturing company accelerated growth among new hires. A manufacturing company tracked performance of salespeople over their first 20 months with the company to understand how quickly new salespeople became effective and why. A key finding was that the quality of the first-line manager (FLM) had a large impact on new salesperson performance. Salespeople reporting to top-performing FLMs performed much better in their first 20 months on the job compared to salespeople working with average-performing FLMs. Top-performing managers did two things that contributed to the performance difference: they spent more time coaching in the field, and they arranged for mentorship from experienced team members. Based on these findings, the company established new coaching expectations for FLMs and implemented a tracking system to ensure accountability.

A medical supply company boosted profits by reallocating sales effort across products. A medical supply company had several products in its portfolio. The amount of sales time devoted to each product varied by salesperson. By analyzing differences in the amount of time that salespeople spent by product and the resulting product sales and profits, the company determined a vastly improved way to allocate sales effort across the portfolio. The company aligned the incentive plan to reflect that effort allocation and educated the sales force about how to spend sales time in order to optimize performance. The result was a measurable increase in sales and profits without any change in sales force head count.

A business services outsourcing company improved performance in nonmetro geographies. A business services outsourcing company compared the performance of its 50 least urban (i.e., nonmetro) sales territories to that of its 50 most urban territories. Sales per territory averaged $1.2 million in both groups. Yet when compared to urban territories, the nonmetro territories had 79 percent more prospects and 49 percent more overall market potential. Salespeople in urban territories visited good prospects on average four times a year; but in nonmetro territories, that average was just 2.8 visits. Salespeople in nonmetro territories were not realizing opportunities because they were stretched beyond their capacity. The company reduced the size of non-metro territories and assigned coverage of many prospects in outlying areas to an inside sales team. This led to increased market share, reduced travel costs, and improved sales force effectiveness outside the metropolitan areas.

A telecom company got more business from its low-performing, high-potential customers. A telecom company took advantage of an emerging way to hunt for opportunities by using a collaborative filtering model, similar in concept to algorithms used by companies such as Netflix and Amazon. The company found "data doubles" for low-performing, high-potential customers—that is, other customers who had a similar demographic profile (for example, the same industry and scale) but who were buying much more. The company analyzed the purchase patterns and sales strategies at these more-successful data double accounts and shared the insights gained with the sales force. The information enabled salespeople to improve targeting of the right products for underperforming customer accounts, thus driving stronger uptake of new product lines and dramatically improving the realization of cross-selling and upselling opportunities.

Together, these examples provide great lessons about how to find sales growth opportunities. It's not enough to look at aggregate performance across the sales force; aggregation hides insight. Finding opportunities requires observing and understanding differences within specific customer segments, products, or groups of salespeople, including differences in the following.

- **Performance outcomes.** Novartis observed that salespeople with similar market potential had dissimilar sales results; it realized opportunity by understanding what those salespeople did differently. Similarly, the manufacturing company observed performance differences across new hires, and the telecom company observed differences across demographically similar customers.

- **Sales activity.** The medical supply company observed that salespeople allocated time differently across products and realized opportunity by understanding how these differences affected sales.

- **Sales potential.** The business service outsourcing company observed differences in territory sales potential and realized opportunity by understanding the impact on sales activity and results.

Companies will always be thinking about their next source of growth. Today's world of big data enables companies to creatively slice and dice historical sales force data to find new and better sources of insight.

This blog was first published on September 17, 2015, on the Harvard Business Review web site:
https://hbr.org/2015/09/how-to-spot-hidden-opportunities-for-sales-growth

Who Owns Your Customer Relationships: Your Salespeople or Your Company?

Your R&D group develops a unique new product. Manufacturing produces it. Finance puts the systems in place to track the money coming in. Marketing designs the promotional campaign. Your sales force is ready to execute. "We own the relationships with customers," say your salespeople. "The company holds us accountable for revenues and expects us to develop and maintain the connections to drive sales. Just pay us our commissions and leave us alone."

A sales model that pays salespeople almost entirely on commission and gives them exclusive "ownership" of customers often works for a while for products in unsaturated markets. With seemingly unbounded opportunity, salespeople work hard to build relationships and create a *book* of business that drives their future financial success and creates fast market penetration for the company. But the "salesperson owns the customer" model is a double-edged sword. Three examples show the issues that can arise.

Sales force complacency and high turnover of new salespeople. At an insurance company, tenured salespeople had amassed large territories and "owned" so many high-potential accounts that they didn't have enough time to provide adequate service and coverage for all of them. These salespeople earned lucrative commissions on sales to current customers and had little incentive to hunt for new customers. With sales slowing, the company struggled to attract and retain new salespeople, who couldn't build a book of business to earn a living. Annual first-year salesperson turnover was 60 percent. Sales leaders tried to realign accounts to help the newer salespeople succeed while improving account coverage, but the top earners who controlled important customer relationships pushed back. To avoid losing top producers and their customers, the sales leaders abandoned their plan.

Runaway pay. A medical device company needed to cut sales force costs. As a startup, the company gave salespeople customer "ownership" and paid a 4 percent commission on sales. In the first year, salesperson pay averaged $125,000. As sales took off, management continued to "share the wealth." After several years, salespeople earned more than $650,000 a year, resetting the pay scale for the entire industry. When competitors entered the market and customers became more price-sensitive, sales growth slowed, and the value that salespeople added no longer justified their pay level. Yet leaders were hard-pressed to cut pay. Competitors were already poaching the company's salespeople, and lower commissions would prompt more to jump ship and take customers with them.

Inability to adapt. As the product line at a technology company broadened to meet the needs of customers seeking comprehensive business solutions, sales leaders planned to expand the company's sales force by adding specialists who could bring technical product expertise to customers. When the company's salespeople learned that this would require them to give up exclusive "ownership" of their customers, they vehemently objected. The sales leaders lacked the will and courage to make the needed change, resulting in an undersized sales force with inadequate expertise to meet customer needs.

The issue of who owns customers—salespeople or the company—is really a question of who and what the sources of customer value are. In the examples, customers perceived the salesperson as the primary value source—the one who listens, assesses needs, provides solutions, and delivers continuing service. But when the situation changes—due to factors such as customers' need for more complex solutions, market saturation, new competition, or a broadening product line—a salesperson alone no longer delivers adequate value. Sales organizations can better position themselves for long-term success by adapting their go-to-market approach to create multiple customer value sources. Here are some ways to do this.

1. **Multiplex to give customers many meaningful connections to the company.** For example, an account manager maintains the customer relationship, specialists provide technical assistance, and service people keep the solution working. All are sources of customer value.

2. **Create tools and programs that add value throughout the sales process.** For example, a web site makes the purchasing process efficient, and tools provide salespeople with insights about a customer's business. The sales and fulfillment process itself becomes something the customer relies on.

3. **Capture account information using a Customer Relationship Management (CRM) or other system.** With a CRM or other system,

people throughout the company, not just one salesperson, can learn the needs and history of each customer. If a salesperson leaves the company, customer knowledge is not lost.

4. **Create a team-oriented sales force culture.** Hire salespeople who are team players. Establish systems and processes that encourage teamwork and the sharing of best practices among salespeople. Reduce commissions and other short-term incentives, and offer more salary or even stock options that reward for longer-term sustained performance. Track team-based metrics, and recognize salespeople not only for quarterly quota attainment, but also for making lasting contributions, say by working together to pursue business development opportunities with long-term payback.

When you create multiple sources of customer value, customers will rely on several people from your company and on the tools and processes that support those people in meeting customer needs.

Making the transition to a multiple-value-source approach is not easy. Companies are more likely to succeed when they use an event that creates an expectation of change (a merger, new leadership, a new product launch, a missed financial goal) as a catalyst for enabling the transformation.

This blog was first published on December 21, 2011, on the Harvard Business Review web site: **http://blogs.hbr.org/2011/12/who-owns-your-customer-relatio/**

Why You Need to Measure Sales Territory Market Potential

If you spend much time around salespeople, it won't take long before you hear them griping about the issue that is the profession's biggest trouble spot: disagreement over the market potential of a group of accounts or a territory. Consider a few examples.

- A regional sales director says, "The Pittsburgh territory is vacant again. This is the fifth vacancy in two years. In exit interviews, the people who leave imply they don't have enough market potential to succeed."

- A salesperson says, "My quota is 10 percent higher than last year. I've already maxed out the potential within my accounts. How am I supposed to get the growth I'm expected to deliver?"

- A district sales manager says, "These district sales rankings are unfair. My district's market potential is below average and is spread across a huge geography. How can I compete with districts in easier-to-cover, more lucrative markets?"

These concerns, and many others, can be moderated with actionable measures of account or territory market potential.

Consider how market potential estimates helped a business within GE that leases over-the-road trailers to trucking, retail, and manufacturing companies. The business had ambitious revenue growth goals, and sales leaders wanted to focus sales efforts on the most attractive opportunities. By using customer profile characteristics (such as fleet size and composition, company size, and industry) to predict customer potential, the sales force experienced a 33 percent increase in qualified leads in one year. GE also used the information to redeploy several sales territories into more lucrative markets. This allowed the business to grow sales productivity by 7 percent and give back a budgeted $2 million for additional head count (the productivity improvements allowed the sales organization to meet growth goals without adding people).

Smart sales forces know that market potential is the keystone for both strategic and tactical sales force decision making. Market potential adds insight to sales planning. For example:

- **Sales force strategy and scale.** If you know market potential by account segment, you can scale and deploy sales resources appropriately against opportunities and can develop segment-appropriate value propositions and sales processes.

- **Sales force deployment.** If you know potential geographically, you can decide where to add sales head count to capture unrealized opportunity and where to reduce head count without sacrificing coverage. And you can create territories that give everyone fair opportunities to succeed. This keeps salespeople engaged and allows the company to hire and retain top sales talent.

Market potential also enables better tactical sales force decision making. For example:

- **Targeting.** If salespeople know account potential, they can allocate their time to better leverage opportunities.

- **Coaching and performance management.** If sales managers know account potential, they can coach salespeople on the best strategies for driving revenue growth. And they can better assess salespeople's performance, provide appropriate feedback, and rank salespeople on metrics that depend on the salesperson, not the territory.

- **Incentive compensation, goal setting, and recognition.** If sales leaders know account potential, they can design incentive compensation plans that reward salespeople for true performance, rather than for a lucky territory. They can set territory sales goals that are challenging, attainable, and fair to all. And they can select the most deserving salespeople for award trips and recognitions.

Many sales forces do not have estimates of local market potential readily available, and developing them requires work and creativity. Possible approaches include the following.

- **Buy existing data.** In some industries, such as airlines and pharmaceuticals, data companies sell information on sales of all competitive products by account or local market.

- **Deduce the data.** If you can't buy competitive sales data, you can likely buy or find data that are a good market potential surrogate. A greeting card company used U.S. Census Bureau data to estimate the potential of each retail store nationwide by looking at population and average household income within a three-mile radius. A company that sold insurance and financing as part of a bundled service offering on retail sales of motorcycles used customer demographics, competitors, the presence of local credit unions, and the onset of spring weather (which triggered an increase in motorcycle sales) to predict territory potential.

■ **Build the data.** You can conduct primary market research to create market potential data. A seller of contact lenses surveyed ophthalmologists across the country to determine the size of their practices and their need for the company's products. You can ask the sales force to conduct market research. A medical imaging company asked its salespeople to collect data on the type, manufacturer, and acquisition date of installed equipment at every hospital and imaging center in their territory.

Knowing local market potential significantly improves sales force decision making. And estimates of potential—even imperfect ones—are better than no estimates at all. Sales organizations that are willing to invest to develop measures of account or territory market potential will see payoffs through improvements in productivity and higher sales and profits.

This blog was first published on April 5, 2012, on the Harvard Business Review web site with the title "Fixing Salespeople's Biggest Complaint: My Territory Is Too Small":
http://blogs.hbr.org/cs/2012/04/fixing_salespeoples_biggest_co.html

Healthy Sales–Marketing Tension

Sales teams and marketing teams pursue a common objective: create customer value and drive company results. But sales and marketing don't always get along. Certainly, all-out war between the two teams drains productivity. Yet having the two teams work in perfect harmony and reach an easy consensus on every decision is a pipe dream. In fact, it's not the best answer.

Some tension between sales and marketing is healthy and productive.

Sales–marketing tension can stem from differences in marketers' and sellers' perspectives. Marketers think in terms of aggregate customer segments; sellers think in terms of individual customers. Marketers design strategies; sellers implement tactics. Marketers focus on analysis and process; sellers focus on relationships and results. These diverse perspectives often lead to conflict. For example, marketing says, "We develop thoughtful strategies that can drive sales force success, but most salespeople won't even take the time to understand them." Sales says, "Marketers are locked in the ivory tower. Their plans look good on paper but don't work with real customers."

But the tension created by diverse viewpoints also has a positive side. It sparks creativity and ensures that multiple sides of issues are expressed. Sales makes certain that customer needs are addressed and that short-term company revenue goals are achieved; marketing ensures that product and customer segment strategies anticipate the evolution of longer-term customer needs. Sales pushes for competitive pricing; marketing ensures that the company uses discipline in pricing.

Sales–marketing tension can also stem from the codependence of the sales and marketing teams.

Especially when things don't go well, situations can quickly turn to finger-pointing. Marketing says, "We worked hard and generated good leads for sales, but they didn't follow up." Sales says, "Marketing's leads aren't worth my time; the last lead they gave us was for a business that shut down two years ago."

But the mutual dependence of sales and marketing creates a productive sense of urgency and encourages both teams to do their jobs better. Sales insists that marketing provide better leads. Marketing makes sure that sales follows up. Sales helps marketing develop strategies and sales collateral that address customer needs. Marketing urges sales to spend time strategically and implement the marketing plan.

Accomplishing the common objective of creating customer value and driving company results requires competency in a wide range of tasks, which fall into three categories.

- **Sales tasks.** Account management, personal selling, distributor management, merchandising, sales compensation design, and numerous other sales management activities typically fall within the purview of sales.

- **Marketing tasks.** Market research, competitive analysis, market segmentation, brand positioning, packaging, and dozens of other market-focused undertakings are usually the responsibility of marketing.

- **Joint sales/marketing tasks.** Sales strategy formulation, lead generation, sales collateral development, pricing, sales forecasting, and many other tasks frequently require the participation of both sales and marketing.

Entire books, journals, business courses, and consulting companies are dedicated to helping marketers and sellers with these tasks. Yet very little is written about how to get sales and marketing to work together to keep all of the tasks aligned around the common objective.

Four strategies help companies accomplish all of this work with a healthy balance of sales–marketing harmony and tension.

1. **Make sure all sales tasks get done well.** Design a high-impact sales organization, hire sellers with characteristics such as interpersonal ability and results-drive, and develop the competencies sellers need to succeed. Support the sales force with structures, processes, systems, and programs that enable sales success.

2. **Make sure all marketing tasks get done well.** Design a high-impact marketing organization, hire marketers with characteristics such as analytic savvy and strategic thinking ability, and develop the competencies marketers need to succeed. Support the marketing team with structures, processes, systems, and programs that enable marketing success.

3. **Implement processes and systems that encourage communication and collaboration.** Ensure that sales and marketing communicate

about tasks that the two teams perform independently, and collaborate around tasks that require joint effort.

4. **Create a culture that facilitates teamwork.** Start with strong sales and marketing leaders who, through their words and actions, consistently reinforce a cooperative, customer-focused culture.

This blog was first published on November 4, 2013, on the Harvard Business Review web site with the title "Why Sales and Marketing Don't Get Along":
http://blogs.hbr.org/2013/11/why-sales-and-marketing-dont-get-along/

Section 2

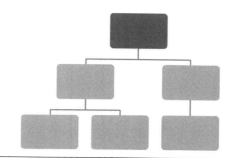

Sales Process and Organization Design

Sales force success requires a customer-focused sales process that maximizes mutual value and trust, and an organizational design that enables effective and efficient coverage of opportunities.

The following blogs share insights about how to design a sales process and organization that align with market needs and company strategies.

Organizing a Sales Force by Product or Customer, and Other Dilemmas

HP announced in March 2012 that it was combining its printer and personal computer businesses. According to CEO Meg Whitman, "The result will be a faster, more streamlined, performance-driven HP that is customer focused."

The merging of the two businesses was a reversal for HP. In 2005, HP split off the printer business from the personal computer business, dissolved the Customer Solutions Group (CSG), which was a sales and marketing organization that cut across product categories, and pushed selling responsibilities down to the product business units. The goal was to give each business unit greater control of its sales process and, in former CEO Mark Hurd's words, to "perform better—for our customers and partners."

The choice—to build a sales organization around customers or products—has vexed every company with a diverse product portfolio. It's not uncommon for a firm such as HP to vacillate between the two structures, but switching structures is not always a recipe for success.

When a customer-focused sales organization supports multiple product business units (as was the case before HP eliminated the CSG in 2005), there is often conflict between the salespeople responsible for customers and the people in the business units responsible for product success. Product people might say: "Our product brings in the profits, yet it's not getting enough sales force attention" or "Salespeople want customer control, but we have the product expertise." And from the sales team: "We are trying to do the best for our customers. The product people are not being team players."

Especially when performance lags, people in any sales structure see and feel the disadvantages and stresses that their structure creates. But they often see only the benefits of the structure that they are not operating in. The alternative looks enticing—unreasonably so.

HP's dilemma illustrates one of many two-edged swords of sales management. These swords are reasonable choices that sales leaders make that have a sharp beneficial edge, but the very nature of the benefit is tied to another sharp edge that has drawbacks. Unless the undesirable edge is dulled, the choice cannot work.

Consider a choice like the one HP made in 2012 to organize its sales force by customer rather than by product.

- **The beneficial edge.** Salespeople can understand the customer's total business, can cross-sell and provide solutions (not just products), and can act as business partners rather than vendors for their customers.

- **The undesirable edge.** Salespeople will have less product expertise and focus, and it will be difficult for the company to control how much effort each product gets.

- **Dulling the undesirable edge.** The company could create product specialists to assist customer managers (although this would add costs, would require coordination, and would work only if salespeople and the culture are team-oriented). It could also use performance management and incentives to manage effort allocation.

Sales is full of such double-edged swords. For example:

- If you hire mostly experienced people, they will become productive rapidly. But they will come with their own ways of doing things and may have trouble fitting into the new environment.

- If you drive a structured sales process through the organization, things will be more transparent and organized, and coordination across people will be easier. But out-of-the-box thinking will be diminished, and managers might use the defined structure to micromanage their people.

- If you give salespeople customer ownership and pay them mostly through commissions, you will attract independent, aggressive salespeople and encourage a performance-oriented culture. But this will discourage teamwork and create a brittle relationship based mostly on money.

Effective sales leaders recognize the two edges of each of these (and other) choices. They work to sharpen and leverage the good edge, while dulling the impact of the other edge. Overly optimistic leaders who see the benefits of only one choice will lead their sales force into peril!

This blog was first published on May 16, 2012, on the Harvard Business Review web site: **http://blogs.hbr.org/cs/2012/05/the_double_edged_sword_of_sale.html**

The Growing Power of Inside Sales

The number of inside sales jobs has increased dramatically in recent years, far outpacing the growth in jobs for field salespeople. We spoke with Mike Moorman, a senior leader in ZS's B2B Sales and Marketing practice and a leading authority on sales management, about how inside sales (which refers to sales positions done remotely from headquarters, without face-to-face meetings with clients) is transforming the way that B2B companies interact with their customers.

Mike, can you give us some examples of companies that are shifting resources to inside sales?

Yes, absolutely. Over the last several years, B2B companies have been ramping up their inside sales investment.

- AstraZeneca has replaced virtually all of its field sales force support for its mature brand Nexium with a 300-person inside sales team. The team provides for most doctors' basic needs for samples and information at a substantially reduced cost.

- IBM has invested in social media training, tool kits, and personalized digital pages to help its inside salespeople generate leads and manage account relationships. Early results include a 55 percent increase in Twitter followers and a significant increase in the number of high-quality inbound leads.

- SAP has refocused its large and growing inside sales team toward working with channel partners, rather than directly with customers, as part of a strategic initiative aimed at increasing channel sales to 40 percent of the company's total sales.

Many B2B companies are making inside sales a priority. I've seen companies investing to create new inside sales teams, adopt advanced analytics to measure and improve productivity of those teams, realign inside and field sales to optimize market coverage, provide value-based selling tools tailored to inside sales, and upgrade their inside sales customer engagement processes and skills.

Why do you think so many companies are turning to inside sales?

Three primary factors give momentum to inside sales. First, B2B sellers feel competitive pressure to cut costs, and they're seeking more efficient ways to sell. Second, B2B buyers are becoming more comfortable purchasing and collaborating remotely; they use the web to research product information, are comfortable communicating and collaborating with sellers using methods such as email, social media, and conference calls, and in fact prefer these methods over face-to-face communication for some sales tasks. Third, new easy-to-use online webinar and videoconferencing technologies make it possible for inside salespeople to create customer intimacy without field interaction.

What types of selling situations or tasks are most compatible with inside sales?

Most B2B selling models include both inside and field sales, and the challenge and the opportunity come in determining the sweet spot for inside sales within an overall selling model. Effective use of inside sales requires partitioning the sales job and dividing it among inside and field salespeople according to some or all of the following dimensions. Different companies divide it in different ways.

■ **By market segment.** Use inside sales for the entire sales process in small to medium-sized businesses that have straightforward needs and moderate to low potential. Use field sales to manage large accounts with complex needs and buying processes and more opportunity.

■ **By stages of the customer engagement process.** Use inside sales to supplement field sales activities in large accounts, especially early in the sales process (e.g., lead generation) or late in the sales process (e.g., repeat purchases). Use field sales for tasks that benefit from a "high-touch" approach.

■ **By products/services.** Use inside sales to sell transactional offerings and solutions with lower buyer risk that don't require on-site assessments or collaboration. Use field sales to sell more complex products and services that require a consultative approach and customization.

■ **By geography.** Use inside sales to reach nonstrategic accounts in remote areas, and field sales to cover accounts in metropolitan areas.

How does increased use of inside sales impact the job of field salespeople?

I see two main implications for field salespeople. First, many companies are experiencing a bifurcation of sales jobs. Inside salespeople are taking over more sales tasks to drive cost-effectiveness. In conjunction, the bar is rising for field salespeople. Buyers are no longer interested in meeting live with "information providers"; they expect field salespeople to bring new ideas and to create and prove substantial value.

Likewise, executives are increasingly reluctant to invest in expensive field sales resources unless those resources clearly provide greater customer and company value. The role and profile of a field salesperson is becoming similar to the role and profile of a key account manager—someone who brings business acumen and problem-solving skills and who can help buyers define opportunities and tailor solutions. Field salespeople need to develop new competencies as consultative sellers, and often companies find that some field salespeople who were successful in the old world lack the characteristics required for success in the new one.

Second, although field salespeople still have a clearly defined role as face-to-face sellers, technology enables them to accomplish more sales activities remotely to optimize efficiency (smart use of time) and effectiveness (impact with customers). Increasingly, field salespeople are selectively leveraging email, social media, webinars, and videoconferencing to maximize their own productivity and enhance customer experience. In this regard, the line between field sales and inside sales is blurring. For field salespeople, this means developing new technology and communication competencies.

What kind of result can companies expect?

When appropriately utilized, inside sales reduces cost-of-sales by 40 to 90 percent relative to field sales, while revenues may be maintained or even grow. Benefits include

- Reduced sales force cost-per-contact and increased number of contacts per day

- Increased revenues in accounts that were lowest priority for field sales but are high priority for inside sales

- Greater access and faster response times for customers

- Increased effectiveness by specializing inside salespeople by industry, product, or activity, without the increased territory size penalty that specialization creates for field sales teams

- Flexibility to scale up the size of inside sales teams without relocation of salespeople

- Better coaching and development for inside salespeople who share a working location with their manager, resulting in shorter ramp-up and more apprenticeship

When focused on the right market segments, stages of the customer engagement process, and products and services, inside sales drives huge sales force efficiency improvements with little or no effectiveness loss. As customers get more comfortable buying in this way, I expect the impact will become even greater.

This blog was first published on July 29, 2013, on the Harvard Business Review web site: **http://blogs.hbr.org/cs/2013/07/the_growing_power_of_inside_sa.html**

Does Your Company Have the Right Number of Salespeople?

For sales managers, this is not an easy question to answer. The number of salespeople affects profitability by impacting both revenues and costs. It's easy to estimate costs by looking at historical compensation, benefits, field support, and travel costs per salesperson. But it's much more difficult to predict revenues, as it requires understanding how complexities such as customer needs, the economy, and the effectiveness of your salespeople and your competitors' salespeople influence a sales force's ability to generate sales.

Most companies use financial decision rules to determine how large their sales forces should be, but regrettably, these rules often lead to poor decisions. Consider three commonly used rules.

Add a salesperson when there are enough sales to pay for that person. This "wait and see" approach to adding salespeople views the sales force as a cost item justified by sales, rather than as an investment that drives sales. An "earn your way" strategy is sometimes necessary in markets with high uncertainty or when a company is cash-strapped. But when leaders take this conservative growth approach even when there is reasonable certainty of success and available financing, they undersize their sales forces and forfeit opportunity. One pharmaceutical company's overly cautious sales force expansion strategy resulted in too little support for a new product launch and cost the company 17 percent of profits over three years.

Split a territory as soon as its sales hit a threshold level. At one company, when a territory hits $3 million in sales, sales leaders split the territory and give a portion of it to a new salesperson. The current salesperson's "reward" for working hard to build business is to have his or her territory reduced. Over time too many salespeople are placed in geographies where salespeople were successful initially and too few are placed in other geographies where considerable market potential remains untapped. Another downside is that salespeople in territories with sales approaching $3 million have incentive to stop selling in order to keep their territories intact.

Keep sales force costs at a constant percentage of sales. A sales force stays affordable by keeping costs in line with industry or company benchmarks for a sales force cost-to-sales ratio. But this is not the same as maximizing profits. Although it's counterintuitive, when a sales force is undersized, adding salespeople increases the cost-to-sales ratio and also increases profitability. You can always reduce the cost-to-sales ratio by cutting head count, but the impact on profitability is positive only if the sales force is already too large. Maintaining an industry average cost-to-sales ratio is especially harmful to small-share companies that want a competitive share-of-voice. Sustaining a historical ratio is also dangerous during a business downturn; it may result in excessive downsizing that amplifies the impact of the downturn and leaves the company poorly positioned for a turnaround.

There's a better approach. Financial decision rules alone are not enough for figuring out the optimal number of salespeople. A better approach requires three steps.

Step 1. Look at four sources for signs that the sales force is under- or oversized. If customers complain about inadequate service, if salespeople protest about too much work and travel, if sales activity focuses mostly on order taking instead of prospecting, and if competitors are expanding their sales forces, it's likely that your sales force is smaller than it should be. On the other hand, if customers avoid returning your salespeople's calls, if salespeople feel they don't have enough opportunities, if sales activity emphasizes too many noncritical tasks and low-value customers, and if competitors are downsizing their sales forces, it's likely your sales force is too large.

Step 2. Do analysis that focuses on customers, not financial constraints. This requires understanding and segmenting customers according to their needs and potential, and determining what sales process and how much sales force time is required to meet those needs and realize the potential. By aggregating time required across customer segments, you can estimate the number of salespeople required to effectively cover your customer base.

Step 3. Look at financial ratios (such as sales force cost-to-sales) as a final check. Adjust as needed to ensure affordability. Often, by shifting coverage of lower-value customer segments to more efficient channels such as telesales, it's possible to improve financial ratios while giving up minimal coverage of market potential.

Finally, keep in mind that changes in sales force size have both short-term and long-term impact. The cost impact is immediate, but the revenue impact accrues slowly and accelerates with time. When expanding the sales force, it takes new salespeople time to get acclimated and make sales, and for the new customers they acquire to make repeat purchases. Alternatively, when downsizing a sales force, loyal customers may continue to buy for a while despite reduced sales force coverage. But eventually, repeat business dwindles away. The best sales force sizing decisions look at profitability over at least a three-year time horizon. If leaders under pressure to deliver short-term results focus only on the first-year impact, they will undersize the sales force—our research indicates by 18 percent on average. As a result, they sacrifice long-term profitability.

This blog was first published on February 26, 2013, on the Harvard Business Review web site: **http://blogs.hbr.org/cs/2013/02/does_your_company_have_the_rig.html**

Does Your Company Have Enough Sales Managers?

A healthcare industry sales executive recently told us that as part of a continued effort to cut costs, her company had reduced the number of first-line sales managers from 66 down to 30 over a period of several years. This meant that management span of control had more than doubled from an average of five or six salespeople per manager up to 12 to 15 per manager. Certainly, the move saved costs, but was it a good idea?

The average span of control for U.S. sales forces is 10 to 12 salespeople per manager, but there is wide variation around this average. At an energy company that sells to large utilities and industrial organizations, sales teams work with customers to deliver technically complex, custom solutions; each sales manager supervises an average of six to eight strategic account managers. At the other end of the spectrum, at a consumer packaged goods company, part-time merchandisers perform activities such as stocking shelves, setting up displays, and conducting inventories in retail stores. The merchandising force operates with an unusually high span of control of 50 merchandisers per manager.

Span-of-control decisions affect sales management efficiency and effectiveness. If sales managers oversee too few salespeople, the sales force incurs high costs and underutilizes management talent. Managers may micromanage their people. They may get overly involved in customer management tasks that salespeople should do themselves. And they may spend too much time doing low-value administrative work. Sales management is inefficient. Alternatively, if sales managers have too many people reporting to them, they can't spend enough time coaching and supervising each person. Salespeople will have unequal skill and quality and will execute the sales process with varied success. Managers won't have enough time to spend with key customers or to develop strategies for driving long-term business success. Sales management is ineffective.

The best way to figure out the right span of control is to first understand what sales managers do, what they should do, and how much time it takes to execute the responsibilities that can't be delegated. Management tasks fall into three categories.

1. **People management.** This includes hiring, coaching, supervising, and conducting performance reviews. Our recent survey of sales leaders indicates that most sales managers spend 30 to 55 percent of their time with people management, but the percentage varies with the span of control as well as with the amount of time it takes to manage each salesperson. Time per salesperson depends on the specific people management tasks, as well as on the complexity of the sales process, the knowledge and experience of salespeople, the quality of sales support (e.g., information systems, onboarding, and training), and the extent to which salespeople are empowered to act without close management supervision.

2. **Customer management.** This includes account planning, customer visits, and assisting salespeople appropriately with important sales process steps and key customers. Our survey indicates that most sales managers spend 25 to 40 percent of their time with customer management, but this percentage varies with the number of customers the managers are responsible for, as well as with the nature of manager selling responsibilities and the size and needs of each customer.

3. **Business management.** This includes sales meetings, budgeting, complying with administrative requirements, and other activities that keep information flowing between headquarters and the field. Our survey indicates that most sales managers spend 20 to 35 percent of their time with business management. The percentage does not vary significantly with the number of salespeople or customers the managers are responsible for, but it does vary by situation. For example, business management time is often greater when sales managers control local budgets and resources or when they must adapt sales strategies to local needs.

Understanding how sales managers spend their time often highlights productivity improvement opportunities. Here are three additional findings from our survey.

■ Too often work with low value to customers and the company creeps into the sales manager's job. This includes many easy but time-consuming administrative tasks. The urgent nature of these tasks prevents managers from performing higher impact (and usually more difficult) duties.

■ Although some business management activities are important for long-term success (sharing market insight, developing local business plans), the business management role is too often a manager time trap. Most managers spend too much time on administrative business management and too little time on people management. The sales leaders we surveyed indicated that, on average, sales managers should shift a half day each week from business management to people management.

■ By eliminating low-value work or delegating it to less-expensive resources, some sales forces have opportunity to increase span of control while focusing managers' attention on higher-value activities.

So is a company better off operating with fewer salespeople per manager or more per manager? The answer is not driven by costs alone; it also depends on management effectiveness. A company needs enough sales managers to ensure that all key management tasks (people, customer, and business) get executed well. At the same time, a company must ensure that noncritical, administrative tasks aren't polluting the sales manager's role. Finally, a company must understand how the role is changing so it can build a sales management team that can drive success today and in the future.

This blog was first published on April 1, 2014, on the Harvard Business Review web site: http://blogs.hbr.org/2014/04/does-your-company-have-enough-sales-managers/

Why Sales Teams Should Reexamine Territory Design

Companies are using more analytics to enable better sales force decisions, yet one area that is still too frequently undervalued is sales territory design, or the way in which the responsibility for accounts is assigned to salespeople or sales teams.

The distribution of customer workload and opportunity across the sales force has a direct impact on salespeople's ability to meet customer needs, realize opportunities, and achieve sales goals. Our research shows that optimizing territory design can increase sales by 2 to 7 percent, without any change in total resources or sales strategy.

So why do companies so often underestimate the value of territory design? Quite often, the symptoms of poor design are misdiagnosed and attributed to other causes.

1. **Is the sales force targeting the wrong accounts?** If a sales force has some salespeople who don't follow up on good leads, and others who spend too much time with low-potential prospects, it could be that salespeople can benefit from better targeting data and coaching. But it could also be a symptom of a territory design issue. If some salespeople don't have enough good accounts to stay fully busy, they may over-cover low-potential prospects. And if other salespeople have too many accounts, they will ignore good leads because they are too busy to follow up and can make their quota by focusing on "easy" accounts. The solution to better targeting may be to redistribute account workload more equitably among salespeople.

2. **Is there a hiring and retention problem?** If there is constant turnover of salespeople in a particular sales territory, it could suggest a need to improve the hiring process or the programs for developing and retaining salespeople. But high turnover in select territories could also be a symptom of a territory design problem. Salespeople could be leaving because they don't have enough opportunity in their assigned accounts. There is a strong correlation between sales and opportunity, and it is typically much stronger than the correlation between sales and factors reflecting

salesperson effort and ability. Salespeople who have too little opportunity will quickly become discouraged, especially if they see other salespeople making lots of easy money milking territories with many large-opportunity accounts. By giving more accounts to salespeople who have low opportunity, those salespeople have a greater chance of generating sales and being successful. This could address a retention problem.

3. **Is something wrong with the incentive compensation plan?** If the same salespeople consistently get the highest incentive pay, even though other salespeople work harder or have stronger capabilities, it could suggest a need to change the incentive plan. But the situation could also be a symptom of unfair territory design. If opportunity is not equitably distributed among salespeople, the metrics that are commonly used as the basis for determining incentive pay (e.g., sales or market share) are likely impacted by the territory more so than by the salesperson. For example, a sales metric favors salespeople with many large-opportunity accounts, while a market share metric favors those with a smaller base of opportunity and fewer accounts. A change in territory design that gives salespeople more equitable opportunity increases the odds that such metrics will reflect true performance differences, leading to fairer incentive pay and a more motivated sales force. Better territory design also enables improved selection of salespeople for rewards and recognitions such as President's Club, while reinforcing a pay-for-performance culture.

Sales forces that have not recently evaluated and adapted their territory design to current business needs likely have misalignments that are keeping the sales force from achieving maximum effectiveness. In today's dynamic marketplace, many factors can cause alignments to get out of sync, including a new product launch, entry into a new market, a revised company strategy, and a new sales force size or structure. To stay current with market needs, alignments need to be reevaluated at least every two years.

Fortunately, today's data-rich environment provides access to all kinds of information for helping sales forces address the problem. A first step is creating a database that captures profitable account workload. Then, by analyzing that data by salesperson, it's possible to identify territories with gaps in customer coverage, as well as territories where sales talent is underutilized. Using a structured territory design process and mapping software, local sales managers can make informed account reassignment decisions that close coverage gaps and better utilize sales talent. In the end, more customers get the attention they deserve, salespeople all get a fair challenge, and it becomes easier to identify and reward the true top performers.

There is no longer any reason for companies to undervalue territory design as a key driver of sales force productivity and performance.

This blog was first published on August 7, 2015, on the Harvard Business Review web site: **https://hbr.org/2015/08/why-sales-teams-should-reexamine-territory-design**

Section 3

Sales Talent Management

Sales force success requires hiring the right sales talent and developing salespeople and managers to excel in their roles.

The following blogs share insights about how to build and develop a strong sales team.

In Sales, Hire for Personality, and Train for Skills

When it comes to hiring sales talent, most companies prefer to "buy" instead of "build." A sales leader at a technology company recently told us, "We only hire experienced salespeople who can hit the ground running." Leaders of these companies argue that hiring experience reduces training costs while allowing the company to gain outside perspective. In addition, salespeople with experience in the same industry bring customers and get quick sales.

But experience alone is not a sufficient predictor of who will be successful in a sales role.

Most companies have hiring profiles that identify the attributes that recruiters should look for. The best hiring profiles are specific to the sales role. Consider two profiles we saw recently for jobs in insurance sales and technical sales.

Here's what the insurance company was looking for in its sales rep:

- Knowledge of industry/sales process
- Computer skills
- High energy level
- Ability to work independently
- Presentation/communication skills

Here's what the technical sales job required:

- Knowledge of business planning and solution sales
- Self-motivated
- Presentation/negotiation skills
- Team player
- Creative/intellectual capability

Some hiring profiles list as many as several dozen attributes. The list usually includes a mix of competencies (learned skills and knowledge) and characteristics (innate traits and abilities). In the insurance sales example, "knowledge of industry/sales process," "computer skills," and "presentation/communication skills" are competencies. A candidate could come into the job with these competencies, or she could learn and develop them after she is hired.

In contrast, "high energy level" and "ability to work independently" are characteristics. These traits are largely inherent to a person. Characteristics are difficult to teach and take long periods of time to develop; consequently, training and development programs have limited impact on characteristics.

Similarly, with the technical sales job, a candidate could learn and develop the competencies "knowledge of business planning/solution sales" and "presentation/negotiation skills" after being hired. But the candidate will have difficulty becoming a self-motivated team player with creative/intellectual capability unless he has these characteristics to begin with.

You can develop competencies with the right training, mentoring, coaching, support, and motivation programs. But to get characteristics, you have to hire the right individuals. In the words of one sales leader, "You can't send a duck to eagle school." According to another, "Although you can teach a turkey to climb a tree, it's much easier to hire a squirrel."

The best sales force recruiting processes focus on screening for success profile characteristics first and foremost. Characteristics should be "knockouts" in recruiting. For example, if a candidate for the technical sales job doesn't exhibit a minimum level of self-motivation, team orientation, and creative/intellectual capability, he should automatically be eliminated, even if his experience gives him outstanding knowledge of business planning and solution sales and he has strong presentation and negotiation skills. Especially when hiring experienced salespeople, it's easy for recruiters to get distracted by competencies. It's nice to have competencies, but you must have characteristics. Without the right characteristics, it's highly unlikely that a candidate will be successful long term.

Bruce Nordstrom, ex-chairman of the department store known for its impeccable service, once said, "We can hire nice people and teach them to sell, but we can't hire salespeople and teach them to be nice." Experienced or not, an individual will only be successful in sales if he or she has the right characteristics—and characteristics are something you "buy" during hiring, not something you "build" by training.

To get those characteristics, you have to hire the right person.

This blog was first published on August 29, 2012, on the Harvard Business Review web site: http://blogs.hbr.org/cs/2012/08/build_your_sales_force_dont_buy_it.html

What Your Best Salespeople Can Teach You

We recently blogged about the importance of knowing what characteristics (innate traits and abilities) and competencies (learned skills and knowledge) salespeople need to be successful. But how do you identify which attributes (characteristics and competencies) belong in your sales success profile?

Perhaps the best source, and one that is too frequently overlooked, is within your own sales force—your best salespeople. Your top performers are very likely to possess the characteristics and competencies that belong in the success profile. The challenge is to identify those sales team members and to isolate and classify the attributes that drive their success. Then you can align your hiring and development programs accordingly.

We recommend a three-step approach—(1) identify, (2) isolate, (3) classify and align—that can help drive sales success by discovering and leveraging the attributes of your best salespeople.

Here are a few things to keep in mind as you execute each step.

Identify. You'll need to identify a group of outstanding performers, as well as a group of average performers (rather than poor performers) to compare them against. When selecting salespeople for these groups, take into account differences in territory opportunity or potential. It's not enough to rely only on performance rankings, competency model assessments, and sales manager input. By assessing territory sales and sales growth relative to market opportunity, you can separate the impact of territory factors from the impact of a salesperson's ability and effort on performance. Most sales leaders think they know who their best performers are. Yet when they factor market opportunity into the equation, they sometimes discover that the success of a "star" salesperson is in fact driven largely by luck (i.e., a good territory) and not by skill and effort.

Isolate. Create a list of the attributes that salespeople use to enable their success. You can look at published lists from consultants and research-based recruiting and training organizations, or you can ask customers and company sales leaders, managers, and HR experts for input. Observe and gather input about the salespeople in the outstanding and average performance groups in order to evaluate them on the attributes. Then compare the results of your evaluation across the two groups to isolate the attributes that truly discriminate the best performers from the average performers.

Classify and align. Your list of discriminating attributes will likely include both characteristics (inherent traits such as high energy level and intellectual capability) and competencies (learned abilities such as selling skills and product knowledge). Classify each success attribute as either a characteristic or a competency, and then align your sales hiring and development programs accordingly. You must hire for characteristics. You can buy (hire) or build (develop) competencies.

The list of success attributes will depend on the sales role. Here is an abbreviated example of characteristics and competencies for a sales force in the healthcare industry.

Characteristics

- Motivated to succeed

- Ability to work with others as a team

Competencies

- Ability to understand customer needs and decision processes

- Call planning and preparation with consistent follow-up

- Ability to adapt the message for each customer and focus on customer value

- Enlisting the help of other company experts in meeting customer needs

With this information, sales leaders were able to focus sales force hiring around the characteristics, and design development programs around the competencies, significantly enhancing sales force effectiveness.

We have seen initiatives like these consistently produce bottom-line results. Global healthcare company Novartis (with whom we've consulted) has been a pioneer in using this approach. Working first with the U.S. sales force, Novartis identified a group of outstanding performers and isolated a set of "success principles" that differentiated their performance. The company developed a new sales process that was derived from the behaviors of the outstanding performers, and it aligned sales hiring, development, and other programs to support the new process.

A key part of the initiative was the development of a selling skills training program called Performance Frontier—The Next Generation in Sales Excellence. The training produced a more favorable perception of the company's salespeople among customers. The initiative contributed to six consecutive years of double-digit top-line growth, well above the industry average. Based on its success in the United States, Novartis replicated the approach globally.

This blog was first published on September 19, 2012, on the Harvard Business Review web site:
http://blogs.hbr.org/cs/2012/09/what_your_best_salespeople_can.html

Think Twice Before Promoting Your Best Salesperson

Do the best salespeople make the best sales managers? Almost unanimously, when we ask sales leaders this question, the answer is "no." Yet paradoxically, and too often, sales leaders look for candidates among the sales ranks and select the best salesperson for the manager job. They assume that because an individual was successful in sales, she will be successful in management too.

Of course, many great salespeople can and do become great managers. But this is not always the case. Too often, when a super-salesperson gets promoted to manager, one or more of the following happens:

- He can't let go of his old role. He takes charge of customer relationships and jumps in to close deals, undermining salespeople's motivation and confidence and weakening their relationships with customers.

- He manages by results only. He expects everyone to produce the same results that he got as a salesperson, but he isn't good at coaching and giving people constructive feedback on how to get there.

- He avoids administrative responsibilities. He becomes frustrated by the many routine but important tasks that headquarters requires of him.

Before long, the salespeople he manages stop learning and growing. They become disenchanted, disengage from their work, and may even leave the company. Soon, district performance is in jeopardy.

What it takes to succeed in sales is different from what it takes to succeed in management. Salespeople succeed when they meet customer needs while achieving the company's financial goals for their territories. Sales managers also succeed by meeting customer needs and achieving objectives linked to company goals. But the manager is not the hunter, the playmaker, or the center of action. Managers contribute to customer and company success when their team of people is successful.

Managers are coaches, not players; they get satisfaction from achieving objectives through others. When a salesperson gets promoted to manager, it's no longer about "me"—it's about "the team." Managers help people grow by walking around with a watering can in one hand and a bag of fertilizer in the other.

Unless you select salespeople who have the characteristics it takes to do the next job well (not just those who have demonstrated success in their current job), your sales management team will be average at best.

What can you do to ensure that the right people get selected for the sales manager job?

Medical device company Boston Scientific has a formalized corporate program for selecting and developing internal candidates for sales manager positions. According to Chris Hartman, Vice President, Central Zone, for Boston Scientific's Cardiology, Rhythm and Vascular Group, "We seek candidates from the sales ranks who have demonstrated excellence not only by generating strong sales results, but also who have demonstrated success in teaching others to sell by acting as a mentor to new salespeople, and who have demonstrated success in managing through exposure to leadership opportunities such as a field training role or participation on a sales advisory board or steering committee. Our management assessment and development program tests and trains candidates on competencies such as coaching, performance management, interviewing, and negotiation. The program provides many opportunities for both the candidate and the company to evaluate fit with the sales manager job."

What should you do if an excellent salesperson who lacks managerial characteristics wants to become a manager and threatens to leave if not promoted?

Sometimes, just talking to the individual about what the manager role entails and what it takes to succeed in the job is enough to encourage an unsuitable candidate to withdraw from consideration on her own. If that doesn't work, test her in the role—perhaps by giving her responsibility as a mentor or field trainer in addition to her sales job. She may discover that the role is not something she enjoys. It's also possible that you'll find out that your initial assessment was wrong. If that's not the case, summon the managerial courage to tell the salesperson that she is most valuable as an individual contributor. It's better to lose one good salesperson now than it is to risk losing an entire district down the road due to ineffective management.

Cardinal Health uses dual career paths as a way to address the situation. "This enables our sales organization to keep many of the best and brightest salespeople who are most valuable as individual contributors," says Sandy Cantwell, Vice President of Sales Operations. "You can succeed by becoming a manager or by becoming a 'super-salesperson.' We have a formal career road map for both management and individual contributor roles. Our top sales role, the strategic account vice president, is roughly equivalent in level to a regional vice president on the managerial side."

Select and develop those salespeople who have strong managerial tendencies for sales management positions. At the same time, understand that success as a salesperson alone is not a good predictor of success as a sales manager.

This blog was first published on July 7, 2012, on the Harvard Business Review web site:
http://blogs.hbr.org/cs/2012/07/think_twice_before_promoting_your_best.html

To Build a Great Sales Team You Need a Great Manager

If you had to decide between having a team of excellent salespeople with an average manager, or having a team of average salespeople with an excellent manager, which would you choose?

Many will argue for the team of excellent salespeople:

- "It's salespeople—not managers—who develop and nurture the customer relationships that drive sales."

- "Replacing one average manager is easier than replacing an entire team of average salespeople."

- "An excellent salesperson doesn't need managing."

Others will argue for the excellent manager:

- "Excellent managers consistently recruit the best sales talent. As they say, 'First-class hires first-class; second-class hires third-class.'"

- "Excellent managers motivate excellent salespeople, develop average salespeople to make them excellent, and keep the entire team engaged and aligned."

- "Excellent salespeople make sales today, but eventually they retire, get promoted, or get wooed away by a competitor."

Clearly, the best sales forces have both excellent salespeople and excellent managers. A team of excellent salespeople will win sales and make this year's goal, regardless of who the manager is. But the success of that team will be short-lived. Eventually, an average manager will bring all of the salespeople that he manages down to his level. On the other hand, an excellent manager will bring excellence to all her territories. An excellent manager may inherit average salespeople, but in the long run she will counsel, coach, motivate, or replace salespeople until the entire team is excellent.

In our experience, companies that have winning sales forces start with excellent managers. Most sales organizations focus considerable energy to build a team of excellent salespeople, yet regrettably, they focus too little attention on building the management team, which is truly "the force behind the sales force." Consider the following evidence.

Role definition. Most companies have a job description for salespeople, and many have a defined sales process specifying how salespeople should work with customers. But too many companies don't do a good job of defining the more varied responsibilities of managers. Managers must play three roles—people, customer, and business manager—so they get pulled from all sides. We hear all the time about "role pollution" in the manager's job. Without role clarity, managers execute tasks that are urgent or within their comfort zone, rather than focusing on what's most important for driving long-term performance.

Selection. Companies devote substantial energy to recruiting the best sales talent, but when it comes to managers, most simply select their best salespeople for the job. Yet what it takes to succeed as a salesperson is very different from what it takes to succeed as a manager. Unless you select salespeople who have strong managerial tendencies, in addition to respectable sales skills, your sales management team will be average at best.

Development. Too often, when sales managers come into their jobs after having been successful salespeople, the company expects them to know how to manage with minimal guidance. Of the more than $20 billion that U.S. companies spend training their sales forces every year, very little gets directed toward sales managers. The result is inconsistent competency across most management teams, as new managers struggle to make the critical transition from salesperson, and experienced managers can't keep up with ever-changing job demands.

Support. Sales managers typically rank third, behind salespeople and senior sales leadership, when it comes to prioritizing sales force support initiatives (such as access to support personnel, resources, and data and tools that enable good decision making and increase efficiency). Rarely do managers get enough support resources for getting everything done—and done well.

Sales managers serve as key points of leverage for driving long-term sales performance. It's a mistake to under-invest in this group. By building a winning sales management team, you can capitalize on a high-impact, tangible opportunity to drive sales effectiveness and top- and bottom-line results.

This blog was first published on July 23, 2012, on the Harvard Business Review web site: **http://blogs.hbr.org/cs/2012/07/to_build_a_great_sales_team_yo.html**

Want Success in Your Sales Organization? Look to the Middle

To build a great company, it's important to have strong executives leading the sales organization. But just as in the military, talented top officers can't make up for weakness in the ranks of frontline leaders, the mid-level managers who are vital in driving day-to-day sales performance. "In any sales force, you can get along without the vice president of sales, the regional sales directors, and the training manager," a sales leader once told us. "But you cannot get along without first-line sales managers."

First-line sales managers (FLMs) are the most critical players in a sales organization because they serve three important management roles—and successful FLMs excel at all three.

- **People manager.** They select, build, manage, lead, and reward a team of salespeople.

- **Customer manager.** They participate appropriately in the sales process to drive success with key customers.

- **Business manager.** They act as a conduit for information flowing between headquarters and the field to keep sales force activity aligned with company goals.

Here are some common mistakes that FLMs make in each of these roles.

As people managers, weak FLMs

- Hire the wrong salespeople

- "Feed the chickens but starve the eagles" by spending too much time with low performers

- Manage by results only and demand improvement without coaching on how to get there

- Take credit for the team's success rather than giving others the recognition they deserve

As customer managers, weak FLMs

- Fail to put customer needs first

- Take over customer relationships themselves and undermine salespeople's motivation and confidence in the process

As business managers, weak FLMs

- Spend too much time on low-value activities just because they are urgent or within their comfort zone

- Put off important tasks that keep headquarters and the field aligned

Sales leaders can strengthen the FLM team and its activities by improving the management support, tools, and training they provide. For example, leaders can enable FLMs in a people manager role by providing coaching tools and training, setting performance standards for how much time to spend coaching high and low performers, and creating a salesperson hiring process with screening tools (e.g., case studies and behavioral interview questions) and training on how to use them. Leaders can also enable FLMs in a business manager role by providing tools and support to make administrative tasks easier.

But most of the mistakes that FLMs make aren't corrected through better management support, tools, and training. Rather, the mistakes are the result of selecting the wrong person for the FLM job—usually someone who was a great salesperson but who doesn't have the characteristics to succeed as a manager. Most successful salespeople, even after they are promoted to manager, are driven by a strong motivation for personal achievement. Unfortunately, this can impede their willingness to

- Let others take the lead with customers, especially when it comes to closing sales

- Show discipline and patience when it comes to dealing with headquarters

- Take a backseat while giving team members credit for success

As a salesperson, you win through your activities; as a sales manager, you win through the activities of your people.

Excellent managers are a must if you want to consistently recruit the best sales talent. Remember the aphorism: "First-class hires first-class; second-class hires third-class." It's hard to recover from bad hiring, which is why it's so important to hire (or promote) the right frontline managers who'll oversee so many hiring decisions.

This blog was first published on January 16, 2013, on the Harvard Business Review web site:
http://blogs.hbr.org/cs/2013/01/want_success_in_your_sales_org.html

How to Make Sense of Sales Force Turnover

Imagine a sales leader who's looking over data from exit interviews with salespeople who've left his company in the last year. Among the departing reps, 32 percent left primarily because of their relationship with their first-line manager, 27 percent left primarily because of inadequate pay, and 21 percent left primarily because of the lack of promotion opportunities.

The question is this: what should the sales leader do to fix this problem?

Is it time to replace or retrain the first-line managers, enhance pay, revisit promotion opportunities—or some combination of the three?

There's more to this story than meets the eye. Let's dig a bit deeper and try to understand who is leaving for each reason.

Consider the following additional facts:

- 60 percent of the people who left for reason 1 (relationship with manager) and 73 percent of the people who left for reason 2 (pay) were in the bottom half of performance rankings.

- 70 percent of the people who left for reason 3 (promotion opportunities) were in the top half of performance rankings.

Most of the salespeople who left because of pay and first-line managers were bottom-half performers. Companies often hope that low performers will find better opportunities elsewhere, so this turnover isn't necessarily a problem. Indeed, perhaps the current pay plan and managers are having exactly the desired effect.

Promotion opportunities, on the other hand, may need attention if the company hopes to hold on to more top-half performers.

Turnover statistics only become useful when they're linked to salespeople's current performance and future potential. Current performance is visible in most sales forces using metrics such as territory sales growth and quota attainment. Future potential is more opaque, but is usually assessed by managers through the performance management and review process.

Salespeople who depart will fall into one of the following three performance segments. You'll want to implement different solutions, depending on which segments account for high levels of turnover.

1. **Low performers with low potential.** These are bad hires, plain and simple. If many sales force departures come from this group, you'll want to find ways to upgrade the applicant pool and enhance your candidate selection and attraction process.

2. **Low performers with significant future potential.** The solution for reducing turnover among this segment lies in helping salespeople become successful through development and coaching and giving salespeople warm leads so that they can taste sales success, which is the ultimate motivator. We find that there is high turnover among new salespeople across many industries primarily because they just can't get off the ground. Training and support that enable early success can work wonders.

3. **Turnover among high performers.** Autonomy, appreciation, recognition, pay, long-term incentives, inclusion on a company task force, and sometimes even employment contracts with a noncompete clause can play a role in controlling turnover for this group.

First-line sales managers are key in diagnosing sales force turnover problems and identifying and implementing solutions for reducing turnover among all three performance segments. Managers are the ones who have to figure out if a low-performing salesperson has future potential or not. They are the ones who must coach and develop a salesperson to realize his or her potential. And they are the ones who can find the right motivators for holding on to high-performing salespeople.

This blog was first published on June 11, 2013, on the Harvard Business Review web site:
http://blogs.hbr.org/cs/2013/06/how_to_make_sense_of_sales_for.html

Section 4

Motivating and Directing Sales Activity

Sales force success calls for a performance-focused and accountable sales team that is armed with the information it needs and powered by the right incentives for achieving superior performance.

The following blogs share insights about how to encourage high levels of the right kinds of sales activity for driving results.

Is Your Sales Force Addicted to Incentives?

A distribution company pays its salespeople entirely through commissions on sales. The philosophy is "you eat what you kill." Salespeople keep their accounts permanently after making a sale. Many tenured salespeople earn several hundred thousand dollars a year, mostly by selling to long-time customers who provide a continuous and stable source of revenue and income. These veterans are basically order takers who feel no urgency to develop new business. Yet as market growth slows, the company can't attract and retain new salespeople because it's too hard to build a sufficient book of business to earn a living. Annual sales force turnover is 57 percent. Sales leaders want to realign accounts more equitably across salespeople to give newer salespeople a better chance to succeed while providing customers with better service. But they fear this will anger top earners and prompt them to leave and take business with them.

Having a highly leveraged pay plan (i.e., less salary and more incentive pay in the form of commissions or bonuses) is not necessarily a bad idea. Executives who receive stock options as part of their compensation have a vested interest in making their companies stronger and more competitive in the long run. What is troubling about the vast majority of sales force incentives, however, is that they are tied to short-term, individual, results-focused metrics (e.g., monthly territory sales). These metrics can discourage teamwork and distract salespeople from focusing on what is required to develop sustainable customer relationships while driving new business and long-term success.

There is a rational argument for using incentives in sales forces. Salespeople drive the top line. If the company can track sales by salesperson, then incentives enable a pay-for-performance philosophy in which salespeople's earnings reflect the value they generate.

Most company leaders will argue that sales force incentives have benefits, yet too often, incentives create more problems than solutions. They can lead to inappropriate, self-serving sales force behaviors, incredible short-term focus, and a counterproductive culture that hurts customer satisfaction and company performance. Consider several examples:

- In the medical device industry, incentives are a large part of sales force pay. Many salespeople feel little loyalty to the company they sell for, as money becomes the primary basis for their relationship with their employer. Salespeople jump ship when a competitor makes a better offer, and they take many customers with them. When two strong district managers at one company left for a competitor, they took with them all of the salespeople who reported to them.

- A technology company had a breakthrough new product but missed out on a significant opportunity when it couldn't implement a planned sales force expansion because several top performers in the company's commissioned sales force threatened to leave if they had to give up accounts (and therefore commission opportunity) to expansion territories.

- In the early 1990s, Sears paid the employees of its automotive repair division a commission on the parts and services they sold to customers. Although clearly unethical, many employees began charging customers for unnecessary work. Several lawsuits ensued, and Sears had to pay out millions to consumers who felt they had been enticed into paying for needless repairs. In the wake of the scandal, Sears abolished the commissions.

Too frequently, sales leaders turn to incentives as a quick fix, while overlooking the power that other sales force decisions and programs have to influence salespeople and their activities and consequently drive results. Incentives are just one of many sales force effectiveness drivers. Too many sales forces today live in the Incentive World (on the left side in the figure below), where leaders view incentives as the primary way to motivate and control a sales force. Most sales forces will be more effective in a Balanced World (right side of the figure) where incentives are just one component of a comprehensive program for influencing salespeople and their activities.

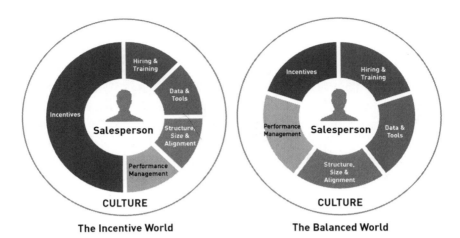

The Incentive World   **The Balanced World**

Overreliance on incentives to motivate and manage salespeople no longer works, given the complexities of today's selling environment. Incentives are at best a partial solution to most of the challenges that sales forces face. By breaking the incentive addiction and developing a more balanced sales management approach, companies can build a healthier culture, create stronger customer relationships, and achieve better long-term results.

This blog was first published on July 11, 2011, on the Harvard Business Review web site:
http://blogs.hbr.org/cs/2011/07/is_your_sales_force_addicted.html

How to Manage Forced Sales Rankings

A vice president of sales recently told us that he drives sales growth by publishing a monthly forced sales ranking of all salespeople. "Salespeople love the competition. They like to see where they stand, what it takes to be number one, and who they beat. Ranking really drives the competitive juices!" But one of the VP's salespeople had a different view of published forced rankings: "My territory covers a large geography that has less opportunity than other territories. The salespeople in big-opportunity territories are always at the head of the leader board. Everybody sees my ranking, but do they ever consider how tough my territory is? I'm sure I'd be close to the top if I had a better territory."

Many sales organizations force-rank salespeople on metrics such as sales, sales growth, or quota achievement, and they use the rankings not only to motivate the sales force but also to weed out the lowest producers and reward the best. Forced ranking helps managers differentiate talent and deliver honest news to salespeople about where they stand.

Most sales leaders agree that forced ranking has value, but what's the best strategy for communicating ranking information? Some, like the VP we spoke with, believe adamantly in publishing ranked lists for the entire sales force to see. Others feel it's best to tell each salesperson his rank privately while publishing only the top of the list. Still others believe that rankings are useful for determining promotions and awards but that rankings should be kept confidential.

Published forced rankings have motivational power, advocates say.

- "Salespeople are competitive. Just like in sports, everyone wants to know where each team or individual stands."

- "Forced ranking makes it clear to everyone what is considered excellent, average, and poor performance."

- "Salespeople will work harder to move up in the rankings. We had one salesperson move from number 73 to number 56 to number 23 to number 3 in just three years."

- "We don't have to deliver bad news. People at the bottom know where they stand on the 'wall of shame.' They get embarrassed, and many leave of their own accord."

Yet publishing forced rankings of salespeople has downsides. There are visible winners and losers. This can create internally focused rivalry, as salespeople soon forget that the competition is out in the marketplace, not within the company among peers. An "every man for himself" attitude develops, hindering the teamwork needed to serve customers effectively and beat competitors. Most salespeople feel unsuccessful unless they are ranked at or near the top. Published rankings make a large number of salespeople feel like failures in a visible way. This risks alienating the "middle" performers (75th to 25th percentile), a large group important to company success. And published forced rankings can diminish the importance of sales manager coaching. Weak managers can allow rankings to deliver the bad news to underperforming salespeople, instead of summoning the managerial courage to have frank discussions that help those salespeople improve.

Whether published or not, forced ranking should always be based on clearly articulated objective criteria and metrics that are accurate and fair to all salespeople. Yet complete fairness is almost impossible to achieve. Too frequently, rankings are impacted by the territory more so than by salesperson performance. When metrics don't account for territory differences, rankings won't reflect true performance differences and can demotivate the sales force.

We believe in the power of force-ranking salespeople and suggest managing the downsides with the following strategies.

- Rank all salespeople, but publish only the list of top performers. This publicly acknowledges outstanding performance and sets up an elite group as a model for the rest of the sales force.

- Ask managers to share personal ranking information with all salespeople who report to them and to coach individuals on strategies for improving their ranking.

- Keep the time period for rankings short so that salespeople can recover quickly from a low ranking.

- Encourage fairness in rankings by using a variety of metrics that give salespeople many ways to win while highlighting the success of those with different strengths and types of territories. For example, one company publishes monthly rankings of its salespeople on five metrics:

1. Total sales, which favors the large sales territory

2. Sales growth, which favors the small sales territory

3. Market share, which rewards the best performance relative to the competition

4. Market share growth, which favors the salesperson who is able to grow share in a territory that is underpenetrated

5. Varying monthly or quarterly metrics (such as individual product growth or new product sales), which focuses attention on specific short-term priorities

Salespeople are competitive. They like to see how they are doing. But they want their ranking published only if they are at or close to the top. A "rank and publish all" strategy risks alienating and possibly losing too many good salespeople.

This blog was first published on July 27, 2011, on the Harvard Business Review web site:
http://blogs.hbr.org/cs/2011/07/forced_rankings_salespeople.html

Five Ways That Higher Sales Goals Lead to Lower Sales

Companies set goals for their salespeople, and most link incentive pay to goal achievement. Many advocate using stretch goals to improve the company's chance of achieving financial targets, reasoning that challenging goals motivate salespeople to think big, be creative in finding ways to create customer value, and attain performance levels never thought possible. But is that always the case? Although some level of stretch in goals motivates, too much stretch leads to goals that are unachievable. Salespeople disengage, and sales come in even lower than if goals had been set at a reasonable level. Unreasonably high sales goals lead to lower sales. We often see company-level sales goals based on wishful thinking rather than on market realities. A higher sales goal can't make up for a soft market.

Five examples illustrate the ways that higher sales goals can lead to lower sales.

1. **Ambitious company executives.** When a computer manufacturer launched a new server line, executives set a company sales goal based on optimistic expectations, not on an analysis of market realities. The goal got handed down to the sales force. Salespeople figured out quickly that the goals were unattainable, and they all but stopped selling the new line to focus on other product categories with achievable goals that enabled them to earn more money. The goal-setting error hurt the company's entry into the server market and made a bad situation even worse.

2. **Systematic padding.** At a professional services firm, the VP of sales added 5 percent onto the company goal to ensure a safe cushion before passing it down to the regional level. The regional directors tacked on another 5 percent before allocating goals to the district managers, who added their own 5 percent safety net. By the time the process got down to the salespeople, the territory goals were 15 percent above the original company goal. Salespeople perceived the goals to be unrealistic, and only 30 percent hit their individual number. Yet at the national sales meeting, the VP congratulated the team for hitting the overall number. The situation frustrated the sales force, many top performers left to join rival companies, and the VP was gone within two years.

3. **Unanticipated market dynamics.** At a financial services company, annual sales force goals were set in a booming economy. When recession hit in the second quarter, it became evident that the goals were unrealistic. By the end of August, fewer than 10 percent of salespeople had any chance of making goal. Salespeople became discouraged and angry that the company was treating them unfairly. Most "checked out" and began holding sales for the following year, when they hoped that goals would be attainable. Leaders contemplated reducing goals midstream to reengage the sales force but feared this would compromise goal-setting integrity.

4. **A flawed goal allocation formula.** Leaders at a healthcare company set a challenging, yet reasonable company goal of 20 percent sales growth. They gave each salesperson a goal equal to 120 percent of the amount he or she sold last year. Top salespeople lamented that the goals were unfair. "I had a great year, so they 'reward' me with a tougher goal, even though I've already captured most of my territory's potential." The discontent of top performers was exacerbated when they saw that their peers with a lower sales base (and therefore lower goals) were exceeding goals easily without working hard. Top performers reasoned, "I'm not going to make goal this year, so the best strategy is to hold back so I get a low goal next year." An allocation that failed to acknowledge differences in territory opportunity created unintentional stretch goals for the company's best performers, alienating this critical group.

5. **"Challenge the stars" logic.** "When headquarters gives me a difficult regional goal, I give a disproportionately large share of that goal to my strongest performers—the ones I can rely on to deliver," explains one sales manager. With this logic, weak performers get easier goals, and the best salespeople are not rewarded enough for their hard work and superior results. Strong performers observe poor performers making more money for less work, and the impact on morale can be devastating.

Sales force goal setting is challenging, given forecasting uncertainties and diverse business conditions across local markets. Salespeople sometimes complain about unreasonable goals for legitimate reasons, but other times they are sandbagging. All sales leaders want to challenge their salespeople to be the best that they can be, and most believe that stretch goals are motivators. When 10 to 20 percent of salespeople miss their goals, the problem is most likely the salespeople. But when the majority of salespeople miss their goals, the problem is the goals.

This blog was first published on September 12, 2011, on the Harvard Business Review web site:
http://blogs.hbr.org/cs/2011/09/five_ways_that_higher_sales_go.html

In Sales Management, the Waning Power of "Push" and "Pull"

Salespeople generally have a great deal of autonomy in deciding which customers and products to focus on, how hard to work, and whom to collaborate with. At the same time, sales leaders and managers try to affect the choices salespeople make using two predominant forms of influence: "push" and "pull."

Sales managers "push" salespeople by directing activities and demanding results. The extreme case of "push" is the command-and-control way of working, where leaders determine what needs to be achieved and how it will be achieved, and they drive processes to cascade their directives down the sales ranks.

At the same time, companies "pull" salespeople by setting goals and providing incentives and recognition for success. By attaching a reward to outcomes—for example, a bonus for goal achievement, or an incentive trip for performing in the top 10 percent of the sales force—salespeople are "pulled" to accomplish those outcomes.

You can push, or direct, salespeople if you know which direction to push. And you can pull if the rewards are meaningful to salespeople and if the rewards themselves do not distract salespeople from critical and appropriate sales tasks.

But because of four pervasive and interlinked threads of change happening in many sales environments today, the power of push and pull is eroding.

First, the increasing democratization of information creates a world in which customers and salespeople no longer rely as much on information from headquarters for making buying and selling decisions. Customers can learn much about a company's offerings online. Salespeople, too, can easily access information about customers and competitive offerings with the click of a mouse. As customers and local salespeople become better informed, the value of "push" gets weakened.

Second, the generation of "digital natives" that makes up a large part of today's sales workforce is communication- and technology-savvy and more team-oriented. The people in this cohort don't rely on a simple vertical conduit of information from their managers. They constantly reach out on their own to get work-related information, often using social media. They are "push"-unfriendly.

Third, in many sales environments, customers are less dependent on salespeople to develop solutions to their problems. Customers are asserting control over the buying process—and therefore the selling process. More and more, salespeople have to collaborate with, rather than sell to, customers. Too much push and pull creates friction and dissonance and little success in such a world.

Fourth, when sales processes are complex or require teamwork, the power of short-term individual incentives (pull) gets weaker. Numerous studies have shown how incentives become a distraction to the completion of complex tasks.

If push and pull are losing their power, then where should leaders go from here?

It's time to step back from push and pull to focus on the person. Just as sales leaders and managers have to adapt to the new realities of managing salespeople, so do salespeople need to adapt to the new selling environment. Success requires a different breed of salesperson: a self-directed synthesizer, problem solver, and team player. The celebrated model of sales success from yesterday—the rugged individualist driven by personal achievement and money—is gone. Sales leaders and managers must build a sales team of people with the right characteristics (innate traits and abilities) for success in today's world. And they must align sales development programs (training, coaching, and mentoring) to help salespeople develop new competencies (learned skills and knowledge). At the same time, salespeople must be armed (not pushed or pulled) with a value-adding sales process and supported by the right tools, resources, and information.

Sales force leaders, managers, and salespeople must adapt to a new way of working; those who can't adapt will not survive. It's time to help the people change…or to change the people.

This blog was first published on December 19, 2012, on the Harvard Business Review web site: **http://blogs.hbr.org/cs/2012/12/in_sales_management_the_waning_power.html**

When Sales Incentives Should Be Based on Profit, Not Revenue

Most sales forces link some portion of salespeople's pay to sales metrics. For example, they pay a commission on the revenues salespeople generate or a bonus for achieving a territory sales quota. This proven pay-for-performance approach motivates salespeople to work hard and drive sales results.

But today, companies increasingly expect salespeople to deliver not just sales but profitable sales growth. Logically, it follows that a sales force can align salespeople's effort with company profitability goals by linking incentives to profit, rather than sales metrics.

When an industrial lubricants distributor started paying commissions on gross margin rather than on sales, for example, the message to the sales force was clear, and the impact immediate. Salespeople curtailed price discounts and focused their effort on more profitable product lines, leading to accelerating margin growth. However, when a medical device company started paying commissions on margins instead of sales, constant change in product costs, distribution costs, product rebates, and portfolio rebates made it a nightmare to determine territory-level margins. The plan was abandoned after just one quarter.

To help you determine whether paying salespeople on profitability is something you should consider, start with two questions.

1. **Is profitability strategic?** Companies sometimes sacrifice profitability for reasons such as building market share, blocking a competitor, or gaining entry into a market. Consider paying salespeople for profitability only if profitability is a strategic goal.

2. **Can salespeople control profitability?** Salespeople who sell a single product at a set price have no impact on the gross margin of sales; the way they increase profits is by selling more volume. Thus, there is nothing to be gained by paying on profitability; the result will be the same as paying on sales. Salespeople have the ability to impact gross margin when they can influence price or when they sell multiple products with varied margins. Paying salespeople for profitability only makes sense if at least one of these conditions applies.

If profitability is both strategic and within salespeople's control, then four additional questions can help you determine the best approach for using incentives to encourage more profitable selling.

3. **Can you measure gross margin at the territory level?** The most straightforward way to encourage salespeople to sell more profitably is to use the approach that worked for the industrial lubricants distributor: pay incentives on territory gross margin rather than on sales. But as the medical device company discovered, measuring and reporting on territory gross margin in a timely and accurate fashion is sometimes more difficult than it seems. Even when information systems allow measurement, complex calculations can make it challenging to gain sales force understanding and acceptance of gross margin metrics. If you can measure and report on territory gross margin at reasonable cost, then pay on gross margin. But if the cost is too great, consider other options for using incentives to encourage more profitable selling (see questions 5 and 6).

4. **Do you want to share profitability data with salespeople?** If you can measure territory-level margins but want to protect the confidentiality of profit margins from customers and competitors, you may want to avoid sharing margin information with salespeople. Some companies have had success paying on margin proxies (artificially calculated margins that reflect the relative profitability of products without revealing actual margins). Yet margin proxies still reveal a lot of information. If confidentiality is a big concern, consider other options for encouraging more profitable selling (see questions 5 and 6).

5. **Do salespeople influence price?** If the cost of measuring and sharing territory gross margin is too great, then linking incentives to average selling price is a good alternative for encouraging profitable selling when salespeople influence price. For example, an office products supplier had a commission plan with a multiplier linked to average selling price performance. Deals booked at more than 3 percent below list price earned the salesperson a base commission rate. For deals booked within plus or minus 3 percent of list price, salespeople earned the base commission rate times a 1.1x multiplier. For deals booked at more than 3 percent above list price, salespeople got the base rate times a 1.25x multiplier. The multipliers discouraged salespeople from conceding price in order to outperform on volume.

6. **Do you want to drive sales of higher-margin products?** If the cost of measuring and sharing territory gross margin is too great in a sales force that sells multiple products with different margins, then paying on sales by product grouping is a good alternative for encouraging salespeople to spend time on more profitable or strategically important products. For example, a technology company created an incentive plan with two product groupings: "strategic products" (newer products with paramount strategic importance and an average 50 percent gross margin) and "core products" (older products with an average 30 percent gross margin). Salespeople earned a 5 percent commission on sales of strategic products but just 2.5 percent on sales of core products. The commission rate differential encouraged salespeople to focus on higher-margin products, thus boosting overall profitability.

Sales incentive compensation plans can play a key role in aligning sales force effort with company strategies. When profitability is a strategic objective and is also within salespeople's control, a sales incentive plan that rewards salespeople for profitable selling can be an effective way to motivate achievement of company financial goals.

This blog was first published on June 10, 2015, on the Harvard Business Review web site: **https://hbr.org/2015/06/when-sales-incentives-should-be-based-on-profit-not-revenue**

There's No One System for Paying Your Global Sales Force

One of the big challenges for the people leading global sales organizations is figuring out the right way to set pay for salespeople who work in vastly different countries and markets.

Some argue that having a single global plan for each sales role (e.g., the same pay mix, metrics, plan type, and payout curve in every country) is beneficial. They contend that a global plan aligns with the needs of global customers and creates uniformly effective and fair compensation. They say a global plan provides control over sales incentive spending around the world, and simplifies plan management and administration.

Others argue that a single global incentive plan per sales role doesn't work. They contend that sales is a local function and that each country has its own market dynamics, business culture, laws, and availability of data for measuring performance. They say diversity makes a global sales incentive plan impractical and dangerous.

When it comes to globalizing sales incentive plan design, companies should tread with caution. Global plan design works only if market dynamics enable similar sales processes and roles around the world, and if countries are reasonably alike in terms of culture, laws, and data availability. Unfortunately, that sort of consistency never happens.

Consider several examples of differences across countries that can create complications for globalized sales incentive plans.

- **Market maturity.** Salespeople in mature markets focus on protecting business with existing customers, while salespeople in growing markets tend to focus on acquiring new customers.

- **Channel structure.** A company might reach some markets with face-to-face selling supplemented by inside sales, and in other regions they sell primarily through distributors.

- **Business culture.** In the United States, for example, the culture often emphasizes individual performance, while in Japan, it stresses teamwork.

- **Laws.** In countries such as Brazil, Mexico, and India, government regulations prohibit reductions in base pay. In other countries, works councils limit flexibility.

- **Data availability.** For example, data capturing end-user sales from distributors may be unavailable in some countries, making it impossible to consistently measure revenue at the level of the individual salesperson.

These issues are typical in global sales forces. It is almost always unrealistic to expect that a single incentive plan per sales role can work globally.

But that doesn't mean you can't make global investments to enhance the effectiveness of a sales compensation program. Consider three approaches that can work.

Develop Global Guidelines

Global guidelines help sales forces in different countries design incentive plans that fit with local needs but also align with a unified company perspective. For example, a medical device company created the following global guidelines for incentive plans for new business development salespeople.

- **Pay level.** Use external compensation surveys to determine what the local market pays for similar sales roles, and set pay level at the 60th percentile, balancing the ability to attract strong talent with the need to control costs.

- **Pay mix.** To determine the proportion of fixed salary versus variable commission/bonus, use external compensation surveys and match the pay mix to what is typical for similar sales roles in the local market.

- **Performance metrics.** Pay on revenues (timing determined locally) for individual (not team) performance; pay incentives rarely for management by objective (MBO) achievement (e.g., for competencies or activities), with a maximum allowable payment of 20 percent of incentives.

- **Performance–payout relationship.** Pay commission with no thresholds (meaning there's no minimum before payout starts), no caps (limits on earnings), and no decelerators (reduced payout rates as sales increase), as these features may demotivate salespeople.

Within these guidelines, sales forces in different countries had flexibility to control many details of their incentive plan design to fit their local situation. The global guidelines significantly improved the quality and consistency of incentive plan design across countries.

Create Centers of Expertise

Global companies can improve sales incentive plans around the world by establishing global resources (e.g., centers of expertise) to help countries design plans. For example, as part of a global sales force effectiveness initiative, General Electric established resources at global headquarters to

- Develop a consistent set of global frameworks, models, capabilities, and best practices

- Propagate best practices through training and education

- Provide wisdom, experience, and project team members who could help businesses execute the frameworks

- Continually improve the frameworks, models, and approaches

The initiative helped GE businesses worldwide assess sales incentive plan effectiveness, improve alignment with pay for performance, evaluate the strength of payout controls, and implement plan change. A project for one business—GE Capital Financing Solutions—reduced the number of plans from 165 to 69 and achieved 90 percent compliance with global incentive plan guidelines that increased focus on pay for performance and profitability.

Centralize Administration

Incentive plan administration is complex and prone to error. Often, sales support teams in different countries don't do a very good job of it. Provided there is sufficient scale, companies can benefit from centralizing and streamlining incentive plan administration. Benefits include

- **Cost savings** by eliminating redundant resources (e.g., systems and infrastructure) across countries and utilizing skilled people in lower-cost labor markets

- **Increased effectiveness** and fewer errors through consistency in data collection and reporting, and the creation and use of operational best practices

- **Risk mitigation** through easier tracking of incentive plan spending and greater visibility into anticipated incentive costs and results by country

When one financial services company centralized sales incentive plan administration, the streamlining of processes led to an 11 percent cost reduction. In addition, distrust of the old systems had caused salespeople and managers to spend as much as 10 percent of their time checking the accuracy of sales data and incentive calculations. With increased sales force confidence in the new system, almost all of the shadow accounting stopped. Sales managers spent more time coaching, and salespeople spent more time selling.

In most global sales forces, cross-country diversity makes it inadvisable to have a single global plan. Yet approaches such as global guidelines, centers of expertise, and centralized administration can do much to improve a global sales incentive compensation program.

This blog was first published on November 13, 2015, on the Harvard Business Review web site: **https://hbr.org/2015/11/theres-no-one-system-for-paying-your-global-sales-force**

Sales Data Only Matter If They Help You Take Action

In sales, as everywhere else in business, there is a buzz about big data and analytics. Vendors hype tools and mobile applications to help sales forces make sense of it all, while touting case studies that generated impressive improvements in sales force effectiveness.

Companies are anxious to capitalize on the opportunity. While some jump in, many are reluctant to move forward. Some will remember or hear stories of failed projects—big investments to give salespeople tablet computers, to develop data warehouses, and to implement CRM systems that ended up racking up huge costs while generating little value for customers and salespeople. We also hear concerns about the newness of the technology or the reluctance to invest in something that might quickly become outdated.

These are valid concerns, but here is the crux of it all. It's not the data and technology that matter. What really matters is how technology, data, and analytics can help salespeople, sales managers, and leaders improve fundamental sales force decisions and processes.

Consider a few examples.

Helping salespeople. Consider account targeting. Traditionally, salespeople decide which customers and prospects to spend time with by examining a list of accounts in their territory and figuring out which ones to focus on to achieve a territory sales goal. But far too frequently, salespeople end up spending too much time with easy and familiar accounts, demanding customers with urgent needs, and friendly prospects. Ease and urgency trump importance.

Approaches that use data and analytics, structured around frameworks that capture the dynamics of customer/prospect needs and potential, help salespeople target the right accounts and spend their time more effectively. Such an approach involves

- Identifying profile characteristics (e.g., type of business, number of employees) that predict account potential and developing an estimate of potential for each customer or prospect

- Using techniques such as collaborative filtering to identify customers and prospects with similar needs and potential (the "data doubles") and to suggest the best value proposition and sales approach for each account

- Closing the loop by providing an assessment of how effective account targeting was so as to inform future decisions

Helping sales managers. Analytics can help sales managers have greater impact as coaches and make more-informed decisions about issues such as sales territory design, goal setting, and performance management. Traditionally, managers rank salespeople on criteria such as territory sales or sales growth, and tie rewards or corrective consequences to these rankings. But if territories don't have equal potential, the rankings don't reflect true performance. Salespeople with rich territories have an unfair advantage, while those with poor territories are demotivated.

Data and analytics enable performance metrics that account for territory potential, so that sales managers can reward the best salespeople, not the best territories. Such an approach involves

- Developing measures of customer/prospect potential, using company and third-party data sources (e.g., business demographics) and sales force input

- Identifying the true best performers using techniques that separate the impact of territory potential from the impact of a salesperson's ability and effort on performance

- Rewarding the true best performers, learning what they do that's different from average performers, and sharing the learning across the sales team

Helping sales leaders. Analytics can help sales leaders improve decisions about issues such as sales strategy, sales force size and structure, and the recruiting of sales talent. Consider how analytics can help sales leaders design a sales incentive compensation plan. Traditionally, incentive plans are designed by surveying salespeople about their satisfaction with the current plan, benchmarking against industry and company historical norms, and checking past incentive costs versus budget. This retrospective approach can blindside sales forces with undesired consequences in terms of sales force effort allocation and financial risk.

A better plan results when companies use data and analytics, structured around frameworks that link plan design to projected costs, sales force activity levels, and fairness under varied market conditions. Such forward-looking approaches improve the odds that despite an uncertain future, an incentive plan will motivate the sales force to focus effort on the right products and customers and be fiscally responsible. Such an approach involves

- Using analytics to test the consequences of proposed plan designs, compare alternatives, and reveal unwanted side effects and financial risks

- Monitoring payout distributions and metrics showing a plan's strategic alignment, motivational power, and costs

- Proactively making adjustments to keep the plan on track

It's not about the technology or the data. Investments in sales data, technology, and analytics can only live up to their promise when sales forces focus first on understanding the dynamics of the *fundamental decisions and processes* that salespeople, sales managers, and leaders are responsible for.

This blog was first published on September 29, 2014, on the Harvard Business Review web site:
https://hbr.org/2014/09/sales-data-only-matters-if-it-helps-you-take-action

Section 5

Sales Force Support

Sales force success requires people, processes, data, and tools that support the entire chain of sales force system outcomes—marketing and sales strategy, sales process and organization design, people, and sales activity.

The following blogs share insights about how excellence in sales force support capabilities can impact all sales force system outcomes and drive results for customers and the company.

Why Sales Ops Is So Hard to Get Right

According to *SPIN Selling* author Neil Rackham, when Xerox first established a sales operations group in the 1970s to take on activities such as sales planning, compensation, forecasting, and territory design, group leader J. Patrick Kelly described his responsibilities as "all the nasty number things that you don't want to do, but need to do to make a great sales force."

Forty years later, the concept of sales operations, or "sales ops," has become widely accepted as essential for effective sales management. With growing demand for data analytics, sales ops capabilities have become an even more important ingredient in sales force success. Perhaps the biggest challenge for sales ops leaders is delivering a huge diversity of work, while operating in a constantly changing business and technology environment.

As an example, a recent job posting on the web site of a global healthcare company seeks an individual for a sales operations leadership position who can do the following:

Strategy

- Contribute to the one- and three-year business vision as a member of the executive leadership team

- Evaluate sales force strategies, plans, goals, and objectives

- Contribute expertise to optimize sales force and territory sizing, structuring, and alignment

Operations

- Oversee sales performance analyses and reporting, territory alignment, and customer profiling and targeting activities

- Administer quarterly sales incentive compensation plans and the goal-setting process

- Manage sales force automation and CRM systems and processes

- Provide data, analyses, modeling, and reporting to support sales force quarterly business reviews

Can one person really handle all this? The diversity of this sales ops role cuts across two dimensions. First, the sales ops leader faces many decisions. The job requires knowledge of a range of sales force decision areas, spanning across categories that include strategy, organization design, talent management, incentive compensation, and sales force automation. Second, the leader must be both tactical and strategic. The job requirements range from tactical/support tasks (e.g., provide data for quarterly business reviews) to strategic/design activities (contribute to one- and three-year business vision).

Consider the competencies required to deliver on some typical sales ops projects.

Strategy. Responsibilities such as evaluating sales force strategies or optimizing sales force size and structure require a deep understanding of specific sales management issues. These activities are best performed by people who have analysis/design expertise—individuals with strong creative and problem-solving skills and project management and collaborative abilities. Such individuals have credibility with top executives and generally crave creativity and variety in their work.

Operations. Tasks such as administering quarterly incentive compensation plans or managing sales force automation systems require specific technical knowledge. These tasks are best performed by people who possess process/detail expertise—individuals who have a strong operational mind-set, are passionate about quality control and efficiency, are technically adept, and generally like structured work, even if it's repetitive.

An individual who provides the steadiness required to be good at supporting operations is unlikely to possess the competencies, such as outside-the-box thinking, needed for designing strategy. At the same time, an individual who is good at strategy probably lacks the process discipline required to be good at operational work. Asking a process/detail expert to do the work of an analysis/design expert, or vice versa, is a recipe for disaster.

What does this mean for sales ops leaders? They must hire, develop, manage, and lead a team of people with diverse and specialized competencies who do fundamentally different jobs and likely have dissimilar career aspirations. The team must not only cover a broad range of sales force issue expertise; it must also include process/detail experts and analysis/design experts working together aligned around the goal of sales force success.

Strategies that use both internal and external (outsourced) resources enable sales ops leaders to build and manage these diverse capabilities cost-effectively.

This blog was first published on December 29, 2014, on the Harvard Business Review web site:
https://hbr.org/2014/12/why-sales-ops-is-so-hard-to-get-right

For Sales Forces, Big Data May Be Overhyped

You've heard the pitch: "You now have a huge volume, variety, and velocity of customer data, sales transaction data, competitive data, and sales activity data. With the combination of cloud storage and computing, mobile technologies, and powerful analytical and predictive tools, you can start mining 'big data' and reaping huge rewards."

It's not that simple, especially for sales forces. We commonly see new technologies overhyped; their capabilities are promoted beyond their potential. Is big data your gold mine? Or is it a mirage that always appears a few million dollars and a few months away?

It depends on how you approach mining big data. Doing it is not enough. You have to do it right.

The history of customer relationship management (CRM) systems holds valuable lessons. The first wave of CRM systems got a boost with success stories in a Harvard Business Review article ("Automation to Boost Sales and Marketing") in 1989 by Rowland T. Moriarty and Gordon S. Swartz. Billions of dollars and millions of hours were spent to build and operate these systems. But as early as 1990, the Conference Board cautioned that half the companies that had purchased CRM systems regretted their decision. In the second wave, led by Siebel Systems, tens of billions of dollars were spent. Many surveys around the year 2000 reported that 50 to 70 percent of these implementations had failed. Now in its third wave, recent CRM efforts are more successful, having matured with the lessons of the early failures and the emergence of industry-tailored solutions that are quicker to deploy and lighter to sustain. But this success has been a long time coming.

So how, then, should you think about big data for your sales organization? Here are three recommendations:

1. **It's not about big data. It's about many insights.** It's impossible to know all the insight types that you can hope for, but it is imperative that you have several to bank on that can help sales force members answer key questions. For example, salespeople can gain insight into which customer to target, which offers maximize value for each customer, and

how to spend their time to drive success. Sales managers can gain insight into what guidance to give salespeople, how to set goals that are fair and realistic, and how to keep a team on course to achieve district goals. Sales leaders can gain insight into how many salespeople are needed, how to attract and retain top talent, and whether an incentive plan is motivating the right kinds of sales activity.

An often-missed prerequisite for answering these and other questions is quantifying the opportunity at each customer or prospect. Doing this, and providing other capabilities that create customer insight, is not intuitive, especially for a team that's naive about sales strategy, sales effectiveness, technology, or sales culture.

2. **Big data behind a sales force is different from big data behind a web site such as amazon.com.** Although the fabled big data leverage of amazon.com and Netflix works in their worlds, the sales world has added complexity. Sales forces are comprised of diverse individuals who know their customers, love autonomy, and are driven by self-interest. To be successful, big data must create customer-level insight that is both valuable and believable to salespeople. It must arm salespeople with information, rather than telling them what to do. It must help sales leaders and managers make big decisions that enable sales team success, rather than simply providing them with a tool for micromanaging salespeople.

3. **You must know what it takes to keep big data alive, healthy, and growing.** Collecting, cleaning, organizing, linking, and updating data are hard and expensive tasks. To understand the extent of these challenges in your environment, talk to others who have been there or who are part of the way there. Learn from their successes and failures. In no area is the adage "Good judgment comes from experience, and experience comes from bad judgment" more true. Before jumping in to join this new technology wave, learn what it takes, and prove some of the benefits in small steps before scaling.

Big data has a lot of potential, much like CRM always had, but we need to do it right.

This blog was first published on August 9, 2012, on the Harvard Business Review web site: **http://blogs.hbr.org/cs/2012/08/for_sales_forces_big_data_may.html**

The Technology Trends That Matter to Sales Teams

The convergence of mobile, analytics, context-rich systems, and the cloud, together with an explosion of information, is transforming sales and enabling buyers and salespeople to engage with each other in more effective and efficient ways. Recently, information technology research and advisory company Gartner compiled a list of the top 10 strategic technology trends. Some of these trends have significant implications for sales forces.

- **Computing everywhere.** Through the proliferation of mobile devices, buyers and salespeople can reach each other anywhere and anytime.

- **Advanced, pervasive, invisible analytics.** By layering analytics seamlessly on top of linked data on customers, sales activities, and salespeople, companies can deliver the right decision assistance to the right salespeople and customers at the right time.

- **Context-rich systems.** Data and analytic insights can be tailored and targeted for the specific situations faced by customers and company personnel. The extreme customization aligns perfectly with how salespeople think and work.

- **Cloud computing and software-defined infrastructure.** These enable fast deployment and at-will scaling of systems to keep up with ever-changing business, customer, and sales force needs.

Consider three examples.

A telecom company developed a collaborative filtering model, similar in concept to predictive algorithms used by companies such as Netflix and Amazon, to help key account salespeople. The model used advanced analytics to make specific recommendations about which products and services to offer to each customer based on analysis of past purchases within that account, as well as purchases in other accounts with a similar profile (i.e., "data doubles"). The model also forecasted the size of the opportunity and the likelihood of purchase at each account. This information improved marketing campaign targeting as well as sales force targeting. Through a mobile app, salespeople could get the information when and where they needed it. Cloud computing and a software-defined infrastructure enabled the system to seamlessly keep up with ever-changing sales force and customer needs. The data and technology enabled the sales force to better understand customer needs and target the right products for the right customers, driving stronger uptake of new product lines and improving the realization of cross-selling and upselling opportunities.

In the pharmaceutical industry, technology is transforming the sales process. A few decades ago, pharmaceutical companies promoted their products almost entirely through personal contact by salespeople with physicians. In 2014, almost half of all physicians put significant restrictions on the time they would spend with salespeople, and approximately two-thirds said they preferred to get information through digital methods. Consequently, pharmaceutical companies now look beyond the sales force to reach physicians. Computing everywhere and context-rich systems allow pharmaceutical companies to get the right product information to the right salespeople and physicians at the right time, using communication channels that include email, social media, microsites, online video, and mobile apps.

In the financial services industry, a company had an outbound inside sales team that sold credit and lending products to small businesses. The company examined millions of phone records and listened to dozens of calls to iden-tify ways to improve customer targeting and sales process execution. Using advanced, pervasive, and invisible analytics, the company performed tests, quickly producing simple, but breakthrough insights. First, by focusing on just 7 of the 14 target industries, salespeople could increase profits by 16 per-cent. Second, by shifting calls to the right time of day, salespeople could triple the probability of a sale and increase profits by 20 percent. Third, by using specific consultative sales techniques employed by top performers, salespeople could further enhance their effectiveness and performance.

Interestingly, the use of technology to improve sales processes is not new. The first "traveling salesmen" used the railroad and then the automobile to broaden their geographic reach. Subsequent generations of salespeople have embraced innovations such as telephones, computers, and cell phones to build stron-ger customer connections. As today's technology trends continue to have an impact, and as new trends emerge, sales forces must constantly and creatively adopt and adapt new technologies to improve sales processes and better serve customers.

This blog was first published on May 7, 2015, on the Harvard Business Review web site: **https://hbr.org/2015/05/the-technology-trends-that-matter-to-sales-team**

Index

mentors 43, 79

metrics 69, 86, 90, 93, 94, 100, 101, 108

mid-level managers 83

Moorman, Mike 58

Moriarty and Swartz 115

motivation 29, 93, 96, 100

multiplexing 46

New York Times 34

Nordstrom, Bruce 73

Novartis 20, 26, 42, 44, 76

number of salespeople 34

Oakwood Worldwide 21, 26

office products companies/industry 101

operations 112

outsourcing 43, 114

Pant, Manish 37

pay for performance 69, 90, 100

pay scale 46

people manager/management (role of sales manager) 83. *See* business manager/ management (role of sales manager)

Performance Frontier 42, 77

performance management 15, 25, 49, 87

pharmaceutical companies 35

pharmaceutical companies/industry 49, 62, 118

pharmaceutical industry 33

poor performers 97

potential 13, 23, 42, 43, 48, 86

price (salespeople's influence on) 101

product-focused sales structure 56

productivity 20, 48

profile characteristics 48, 73, 75, 107

profit (basing incentives on) 100

profit growth 42

promotion (of salespeople) 79, 86, 93

pull 98

push 98

Rackham, Neil 112

rankings (of salespeople) 48, 49, 86, 93, 94, 108

recognition programs 29

recruitment (of salespeople) 26, 72

retention (of salespeople) 14, 68, 69

role definition 82

role pollution 28

SAAS (software as a service) 36

salaries 90

sales effort allocation 28

sales force academic articles 20

sales force books 20

sales force complacency 45

sales force complexity 19, 22

sales force costs 19, 45, 62, 65

sales force effectiveness drivers 12, 13, 15, 17, 22, 23

sales force empowerment 19

sales force evolution 25

sales force scale 25, 49

sales force size 25, 34, 62

sales force strategy 49, 112

sales force structure 25

sales force topics 20

sales force transformation 21

sales process 25, 42

sales process tools 46

sales strategy 23

sales tasks 52

About the Authors

Andris A. Zoltners is a professor emeritus of marketing at Northwestern University's Kellogg School of Management and a co-founder of ZS Associates. He has personally consulted for companies all over the world, helping them develop and implement sales strategies that drive results. He has spoken at numerous conferences and has taught sales force topics to thousands of executive, MBA, and Ph.D. students. He received his Ph.D. from Carnegie Mellon University.

Prabha K. Sinha is a co-founder of ZS Associates and a former faculty member at Northwestern University's Kellogg School of Management. He continues to teach sales executives at the Indian School of Business and the Gordon Institute of Business Science in South Africa. He has helped firms all over the globe with improving sales force strategy and effectiveness. He received his Ph.D. from the University of Massachusetts and graduated from the Indian Institute of Technology, Kharagpur.

Sally E. Lorimer is a business writer. As a former ZS principal, she helped clients implement strategies for improving sales effectiveness and performance. She has an MBA from Northwestern University's Kellogg School of Management and is also a graduate of the University of Michigan.

Also written by the authors:

Building a Winning Sales Force
(2009, Amacom Books/American Management Association)
This practical guidebook shares a proven framework for assessing how good your sales force is and suggests high-impact solutions for boosting sales and profit performance.

The Power of Sales Analytics
(2014, ZS Associates)
This book shows sales leaders how to use analytics, data, and technology to improve fundamental sales force decisions and create competitive advantage. advantage.

Building a Winning Sales Management Team
(2012, ZS Associates)
Written with input from 19 successful sales executives from leading companies, this book highlights the pivotal role of the first-line sales manager in driving profitable growth.

The Complete Guide to Sales Force Incentive Compensation
(2006, Amacom Books/American Management Association)
This detailed guide is packed with hundreds of real-life examples of what works and what doesn't when it comes to creating a sales incentive compensation program that drives results.

Sales Force Design for Strategic Advantage
(2004, Palgrave Macmillan)
This book demonstrates how the right sales force design—including customer segmentation, go-to-market strategy, sales roles and structure, and territory design—gives you a competitive edge.

Coming in 2017

Addressing Today's Toughest Sales Compensation Issues
Learn about the top challenges faced by sales compensation professionals today, along with practical suggestions for addressing them. The authors discuss the impact of changing sales roles on compensation, how to design plans that drive profitability, and how to design effective global plans, among other challenges.

Manufactured by Amazon.ca
Bolton, ON

24131090R00072